RELENT

The Death March

to

Educational Excellence

Considering dysfunction

in our primary schools

BY THE SAME AUTHOR

Poetry
Makers and Destroyers
Love's Troublesome Journey
The Sex Doctor
Scotland's Saint
Wrong Ticket Home
Surveying the Wreckage
Let's go ahead, then!
Epiphany in Azure: Columba on Iona
Likabehandlingsplan: Sweden Considered in Verse

Education Series
The Belt Room
Curriculum for Excellence
Queens of the Reich

Biography
William Wallace
Robert the Bruce
Janet: A Life in Verse

Relentless

Glenn Telfer

Certain that someone out there likes this stuff

Published By
Big Ride
6/3 Pinkhill Park
Edinburgh EH12 7FA
Scotland

LEGAL DISCLAIMER
As a product of the author's imagination, any resemblance to
actual persons or events is entirely coincidental. Really.

A catalogue record for this book is available
from the British Library.

ISBN: 978-1-909297-26-5
e-pub 978-1-909297-27-2

Cover design by Glenn Telfer

Design by Wordsense Ltd, Edinburgh

Printed by CPI Group (UK) Ltd, Croydon, CR0 4YY

Contents

Foreword

What's happening to our primary schools?

How to begin?

Let's start with an observation containing the question; how in the light of all our ambitions, all the funding, all the input of the wise, all the dedicated bureaucracies and ongoing attention and concern, did things become so enervated?

How to define and address the claim that our education system is so stressed and dysfunctional and dishonest?

How to do this without hyperbole, the natural idiom of the complainer?

Such a task would be a gigantic one, requiring a scholar of rare skills and fortitude. They would need to understand the big picture of societal trends while being able to zoom into the minutiae of public policy and classroom practice. This is a task only fit for an intellectual conquistador whose forensic skills and clarity of expression was matched by their courage, for in telling the truth they would make enemies. Such a person is not me.

None of the requirements for the task fit within the constraints of my time, temperament or intellect. And so, caring as I do, I adopt the approach that's mine. My intent is serious, for this is a serious issue, although my methods are whimsical. Indeed, I contend that much of the nonsense which blights the institution is only worthy of mockery.

However, scholarly approaches have been well covered over the years. The learned articles and books, the research (or 'research') with its recommendations, the politicians 'listening' and 'learning lessons'; and they have made 100% no improvement. Indeed, the effect of the various efforts has usually been the exact opposite of the intention.

As our society is losing its values and focus, so too our institutions of education. And first on the list is our primary schools. The slow betrayal firstly by ourselves, then politicians, academics, bureaucrats, managers and teachers continues apace. This is the dynamic of decay. We are all complicit. But if this is how it is, why bother?

As the Roman captain observed of his attempts to persuade Christian convert Lavinia to save herself from a martyr's death, *I knew it was no use; but one tries in spite of one's knowledge.*

I'll have my go at making the same.

Glenn Telfer
Edinburgh, July, 2017

Chapter 1

Some Home Truths

SOME HOME TRUTHS ABOUT EDUCATION FOR TEACHERS

They're not fixing it.

It will never be fixed.

They will never leave you alone.

No one cares about your welfare.

They are not listening, nor learning lessons.

Funding will go to those who have caused the problem.

But you will get the blame.

Teaching is a demon of a job which will devour all your time and whose quenchless lust for control of your mind will destroy your sanity. It can't help its monstrous nature.
'Aphrodite' (former primary school teacher now much appreciated cage dancer at Hell's Belles)

THE CURSE OF FRANKENSTEIN

We quickly tire of our discoveries and hand them over to people
who are not ready for them.

Professor Bernstein

On the one hand, genius and enterprise
on the other, an ethical lacuna and hubris
all combined in his one brilliant personage
referencing this unfortunate balance of parts
he was warned of the looming threat

to his sanity, liberty and salvation:

Can't you see it will all end in evil?
As a scientist, as a learned man, as
the most clever person he knew,
of course, Frankenstein couldn't see it.
Now, why do you say that?, he replied.

Knowing he was making the world
a better place, but not knowing
that he actually wasn't in real life.
Clever is good, too clever equals stupid.
We too in education have our Frankensteins

trying to create the perfect pupil
from disparate parts of unsourced
learning theories, junk science,
new age psychobabble, Third World Guilt
and curricula cobbled together

from the various charnel houses
and educational graveyards
of the global digital dungeon
sorryingly leaving no space in our laboratory
for intuition and common sense

and so, for all their intelligence and
enterprise, our educational barons, like
their infamous template, add nothing to
human improvement while creating a
monster of confusion.

However, they have learned from the baron, one lesson really well;

that, alas, of hubris, as demonstrated by
our famous Curriculum of Excellence.
And now the truth, Hubris summoning Nemesis,[*]
as our educational experts lead us into the vortex
of their making, all we are waiting on is the fall.

*"...You must choose between the flames and the police,
Frankenstein."*

---

[*] as it always does

Chapter 2

Remembering the Slate Scratchers[*]

---

* In contrast with the ironic detachment hopefully exhibited elsewhere in this work, this chapter is written with a sincere respect for nearly all my old teachers.

REMEMBERING THE SLATE SCRATCHERS

iPadders are you ready? Slate scratchers are you ready?
Contestants begin!

How could they do so much with so little?

They, our European ancestors, built the modern world we live in. Or, for those others around the world, the one they want to live in. They invented and developed things, arts, concepts and working systems that generally made the world a better place. This progress towards a higher civilisation was certainly not a smooth road. But bit by bit, comfort and security, and the ideas and institutions which sustain them, have increased. So too, fairness and possibility in your own life. This I take as self-evident.

Much, possibly most, of this recent transformative power traces its origin to our ancestors' formal education. This itself a consequence of the various 19th century education acts which, building on earlier church and private initiatives, established our modern state school systems. And yet, while successfully providing a society-wide education, actually *what* they provided often seems to us now a crude and limited thing, replete with prejudice and cruelty, and taking place in primitive surrounding. How, then, given the lack of most of the techniques, resources, technologies and correct attitudes which we deem minimal essentials for learning, did they build mighty bridges, run complex timetables with precision, write and perform great art, legislate and create immense welfare systems, perfect the mechanical arts, (the machine gun, a personal favourite, springs to mind), create gigantic factories, threaten the world's survival, go to the moon, to name but a few achievements?

A question which occurs is how much this successful industry and enterprise has to do with formal, public schooling in its widest sense, as opposed to dedicated craft training, or even just immersion in a trade? Or, can you even think it out loud, intelligence? To give an extreme example, the people who designed Chartres Cathedral did so without the benefit of a university degree in architecture. And the builders, mostly illiterate. I acknowledge the relevance of this questions whilst I duck it. I'm concerning myself here with what happens in our schools; this is where we and our near ancestors learned what we call an education.

So, do we think we're better than them?

Us on a smart board, them on a blackboard. Us with an iPad, them with a slate and nail. Us with a print off Twinkle sheet to stick into a jotter, them with a pencil to write out the same. Us fessed up with correct attitude and sensitivities, them with plain talking and home truths.

And in asking the question, we already know the answer.

So then, how did these slate scratchers do this so well?

And, if this connects to their education in school, then how? If not so, then why?

SCHOOL MORNING

1961

I don't hear an alarm, just the noise of the grate being cleaned and the snap, crackle and pop of the fire taking. Then, the faint warm smell of it, the glow pulsing on the ceiling, the gentle cascade of porridge making sounds. That's my porridge. Glazed with sugar, floated on milk and all eaten. My breakfast drink, tea (two sugars). Then dressed, kissed and sent to school. Which journey takes about one minute from door to playground.

Run around the playground; chasing girls, kicking a ball, tig, and just running but don't know why. Next the school bell, rung by hand. Efficiently, line up, the volume dial turned to zero in seconds. Boys and girls in separate platoons are quickly marched in to cloak rooms and then classroom where they wait standing in silent attention behind their desks. Waiting for Mrs MacKay. She comes in, boys salute crisply, girls curtsey elegantly, she greets us which we return in unison; children used to be imprinted for such behaviour? The class is led in The Lord's Prayer. Hands and nails checked for cleanliness. Then, *You may sit.* Our hands basketed on the desk. The Bible is brought out and the day's first lesson begins. Her Majesty's looks down approvingly from the wall. No words of censure are required. No-one needs the toilet.

2016

Awake enervated by a nightshift of digital life. No matter when you get up from bed, you're already chasing your tail. Let's make the breakfast modern; maybe none at all, or Pop Tarts, fizzy drink, strong coffee. Jousting with traffic and traffic lights, every day feels like being late.

Children line up at the bell, but without precision and are not easily able to stand quietly, if they can do it at all. You could shout at them for a few seconds of compliance, if that's how you wish to start the day.

The failure to discern the need to alter modes of behaviour in school time carries on into the classroom and through the day with chatting, footering, walking about, constant toilet needs, drinking and spilling of water, and sundry other interruptions. Less focus than a chimp at a tea party.

All these disruptions officially mandated and widely held as necessary features of the child-centred approach by the teachers themselves. The rights of the child as defined thusly held as paramount.

OUR OLD TEACHERS: PART 1

How do we remember them?

12 vs 12

As wonderful record keepers.
As great photocopiers.
As cutters and pasters of Word documents.
As someone who put on Newsround.
As purveyors of purple mash and dojos.*
As stickers of pre-prepared Twinkle worksheets in jotters.
As attendees at relentless junk and propaganda workshops.
As enemies of the patriarchy and the glass ceiling.
As someone whose spare time preferences were twitting and tweeting.
As unwitting transmitters of the civic virtues of former civic dis-virtues.[1]
As glove puppets for global cultures and Pied Pipers of our own cultural demise.
As great GIRFECkers.[2]

Or

The kind word.
The interest shown.
The genuine compliment.
The look of approval.
The necessary speaker of hard truth.
The seeker after fun.
The light-hearted presence.
The representative of adulthood.
The firm justice.
The reliable presence.
The lover and transmitter of native high culture.
The doer of human things.

---

* No, it's not a dinner.

Aye, I know that nothing on the first list need be incompatible with the second. And too that the first list is seen through a jaundiced eye while the second wears rose-tinted lenses. Try swapping the lenses if you think it will make a difference!

OUR OLD TEACHERS: PART 2

What they didn't have,...

Computers, equity, school bomb plan
Cut and Paste, core values, walls falling down[3]
race bad-think, school website

adverts and propaganda (aka lesson resources)
pupil peanut allergy plan, Adderall
individual ipads, hate crimes, Ritalin

smartboard, gender action programme
learning powers focus, enterprise
love of cultural enrichment, Epi pens

learning protocols, photocopiers
Newsround, folios of excellence
targets, anti-bully policy, UN rights

inclusion, schizophrenic enemy press
parental twits and tweets, FGM,
ILPs, PPSs, QIOs, EALs, PSAs, ASLs, PPKs[4]

tolerance, saving the environment
GTCS enhancing professionalism[5]
WWW, overcoming stereotypes

Self-harm, neglect, poverty,
Anti-radical and suicide awareness
'Failing our Families', ADHD

pupil i account closed:
inappropriate content search
contact administrator

learning conversations, dojos
safe spaces, pupil hydration strategy
resilience super powers, fidget toys

gender corrected environment
army of chiefs at Council HQ
3rd World guilt, 66 67 68 passwords

WALT and WILF (although yes to Walt and Wilf)[6]
Islam, steps to growth, active learning
poverty awareness, joined up thinking

password updates, download,
uploads, security warnings,
access denied, cannot contact server,

Excellence.

OUR OLD TEACHERS: PART 3

And, the alternative argument:

*Shut up you boring moaner. This is what the job is and always
was. If you don't like it, go somewhere else. I hear Burger Queen
are recruiting lavvy cleaners.*

Plain speaking former HT, now happily domiciled at the Total Inclusion Care Centre, Block F,
HMP Barlinnie, Glasgow

THE HEAVENLY TWINS

Another loss to our modern age

The magic pairing
of these heavenly twins
sarcasm and corporal punishment
no point in being sarcastic now
as nae belt to back it up!

D'ye know why you're getting the strap?
No, Sir.
See if you can work it out while
your hands cool and
it'll save me doing it again.

---

* corporal punishment in the Scottish style using a specially designed very thick leather belt brought down in a manner resembling a sabre slash from horseback onto the receiving pupil's upturned palm. A considerable amount of force was applied (although only when a boy was being punished!)[7] and sometimes a terrific amount. The delivery occasioned a sharp crack somewhat like a small calibre pistol fired indoors. Insouciance was the preferred attitude of both deliverer and receiver; often both would, of necessity, become studied in striking this stage pose.

See Ian in *The Belt Room* for an example of such a pupil expert.[8]

☞ THE MORE PLUGGED IN...

Only a slave is available all the time.

...THE LESS IMPORTANT YOU ARE 👍

Hand over your life in exchange for your chains. ☺

**FOR MORE INFO:
TEACHER-SLAVE @ SCOT. EDUC 24/7.COM**

With apologies to God, accepting his availability inhabits a unique category

CURRICULUM FOR EXCELLENCE: CELEBRATING ACHIEVEMENT

The brick collected from the bottom of the pool
the float made from trousers, and a classmate rescued
and pumped dry as per training.

After eight weeks practice, the recognition;
lined up pool-side for the society's representative
to personally shake our hands.

The 'Well done!' and accompanying badge
reinforced two weeks later at assembly
with a name-bearing medal handed

out personally in a little ceremony overseen
by our colonel head-teacher.
Public recognition of our achievement.

Glory feels like this in 1969.

Nearly fifty years later, the same children
leave the pool at the last session to,…nothing.
The society's representative replaced

by an internet link by which (eventually)
allowed the class teacher to download a certificate
which they can print out in their own time

to be given out when you find the time,
or whenever! Who cares anyway?
The magic link by which

a real success was recognised by a neutral
whose presence exclusively confirms
the achievement, broken and gone.

The *gloire* clouded over by the cloud
of the internet.
The VIP line-up replaced by a download link.

Glory feels like this in 2014.

Degrading the achievement when
you degrade the ceremony and
societal approbation denuded of value.

So many false distinctions rewarded weekly
and this real one rationalised to oblivion,
this is how we celebrate achievement in our end of days.

Here's the link to download a PhD, by the way:
www.Celebratingachievement/CfE.2014/FU2

ARISTOTLE REFLECTS ON SCOTTISH PRIMARY EDUCATION

And particularly the vexing question of whether things are better now than when he was a schoolboy

HE STARTS WITH A QUESTION: In what way are modern teaching methods superior?

HE HEARS THE RESPONSE: They incorporate all the advances in the various sciences of education and policy practice.

HE ASKS FOR EVIDENCE: Can you justify this statement with examples?

SILENCE GREETING THE QUERY, HE REFRAMES: Tell me one piece of pedagogic research that you have recently considered and which influenced your thinking and actual practice?

SILENCE CONTINUES, HE REFRAMES AGAIN: Okay, not recently, ever!

HE REACHES A PROVISIONAL CONCLUSIONS: The continuing silence loudly suggests an unspoken truth regarding the practical use of 50 years' worth of pedagogic science.

HE INTRODUCES A HYPOTHESIS: Education, like life, is a zero sum game. Something done equals something else not done.

HE CONTINUES: And so, the time devoured by pedagogic nonsense and CPDs* is gone forever. This time is stolen from sanity as the humours have to constantly readjust against the unbalancing forces of fraud and irrelevance.

---

* Continuous Professional Development: Mostly useless, but sometimes pernicious, training courses one is obliged to attend, often with unintended ironic content. The better ones have tea and biscuits.

HE CONCLUDES: Old school teachers had to learn their craft and gradually incorporate wisdom and wit up to their ability level. New school teachers, alas, have to incorporate or marginalise truckloads of junk that daily assault their solemnity and routine.

THE JUDGEMENT: I consider my education superior. My teachers wiser, their spirits all the lighter for not being burdened with the projects of fools, charlatans and office slaves.

We are

what we

repeatedly

do.

For the poor modern teacher it's a...

ZERO SUM GAME

All the rubbish you must do

EQUALS

all the things you should do.

Chapter 3

Zersetzung

THE STASI: SWORD AND SHIELD OF THE PARTY

An apt analogy!

When you're out at work they secretly gain access to your house and...

put a light on,
empty some milk out of the carton,
steal a bill or a membership card,
reorganise your record collection and scratch your favourite,
steal a new sock or a tie.

Ditto at work and other random events in your life. Anyone cognisant of this activity, who may be tempted in a passion of conscience to reveal their knowledge, would be bribed or threatened, in East Germany this was the same thing.
The victim keep's thinking, *That's funny, I'm sure I left my...on the...* They sleep fitfully as they replay the confusions and daily additional slights.
Every day they become more stressed, increasingly thinking that they are going mad. Which they are, of course, but by state design; hence zersetzung (decomposition).
Thus, do they gain control of you, thus do they maginalise your presence, thus do they limit the threat of the truth you represent...and thus do they justify their existence and salary. They know that they are frauds and agents of a corrupt system, and that you are not; and thusly do they hate you.

Zersetzung is a real thing. The former GDR, following on the style of their Soviet overlords, preferred a neo-brutalist approach to wrongthinkers. We in the West naturally make our version an industry and oblige the victim to pay, via debt engineering, internet and TV, for the privilege of destroying themselves.

THE SCOTTISH EDUCATIONAL STASI: THE SWORD ~~AND SHIELD~~ OF THE CURRICULUM PARTY

In teaching we have our own tinpot Stasi spread throughout the educational republic, embedded in ministries and served by dedicated officers absolutely committed to whatever and full pension. The smoke and mirrors of the curriculum could not function without them.

Here is an exert from their brochure:

Enforcement of Educational Goals

Especially selected for their pre-existing commitment to education for justice, our agent candidates are then trained in mind-bending, bureaucratic excess and zersetzung. Once qualified they are then fully equipped and funded to carry the fight for fairness and inclusion into the classroom. A particular specialisation is the use of IT to remotely crush teacher confidence.

Previously rejected by the Gestapo for cruelty, our QIOs and GTCS agents are ideologicaly motivated to lead the charge against curricular apostasy.

Our commitment to fairness is demonstrated by the overwhelming proportion of non men in our profession.

While you are at work our tinpot Stasi secretly gain access to your education department and school management and begin zersetzung:

OLIs—targets—risk assessments

Eyes on the wall—reviews—CAT sessions

Twilight workshops—QIOs—tech errors

Threatened HMI visits—reflective journal—CPD

Security concerns—folios of excellence—GIRFEC

Opposing racism—cultural sensitivity—disability

Sexism—transgender awareness—professional update

LGBT positive-culture of tolerance—mainstream inclusion

Good is not good enough—learning powers—SEAL maths

Poverty attainment gaps—girls in STEM—glass ceiling

Celebrating growth—enterprise—one world justice

IT updates—Assembly Spy—No Child Left Behind

TARGETS

Good shot! Right in the bullseye; you've killed it

Group targets, table targets, individual
targets, planning targets, targets displayed
on the wall and sticky target labels
on evidence folders (*Breath slowly, now!*).

All Learning Intentions and Success Criteria
should be differentiated and linked
to individual pupil targets.
And recorded as 'I can…' and

'What I will do next' statements
after review at the end of the lesson
in Reflection Time.
Teachers should provide pupils

with target bookmarks and
little cardboard bracelets of targets
in the off chance their targets,
God forbid!, slip from their minds.

All this helps our infants formulate their
'What I have learned' statements:
What have I done, How did I do it,
How do I know, What will I do next.

How can I improve?
How can I further improve?
Take that question into therapy
at eight years old!

Good practice indicates that teachers
should produce interim targets
for children's learning, and share
these targets openly

in a variety of ways
that will be 'meaningful for them,'
which last statement I presume to mean
that we finally arrive at the butts.

There is a methodology using targets
that is capable of reviving
those children lost to childhood;
Let's start at 20lb draw and see how it goes.

My father always taught me to put myself into the body of the bow, and not pull with the arms as the French or Italians do.

A MOST DESERVED DISTINCTION

The best fighter, the cleverest,
fastest, fattest, most belted;
I could easily name them in 1966
and none of them were me.

Finding middle level in all,
but secretly seeking distinction
by finding new categories to add
to this important school list;

1 litre cider lunch slugged and
then Bunsen burnered my hair
on the same day to earn a fame
that undoubtedly impressed the girls,

hiding teachers' chalks and
gluing desk lids shut, and (once) the
'most improved diddy' prize in English.
These though were just small things

that nudged me up the scale,
but temporarily, alas never able
to find the circumstance or will
to escape mediocrity

I surrender the big categories
to others and live in modest
expectation of nothing in particular
until Karma

probably admiring my patience
grants a lifelong wish and,
when finding me still in school,
(TBF, I had left it for a while)

decides to make it apt, and then
picks a colleague as the conduit.
And so, us discussing the conduct
of a boy now identified as 'challenging'

in whatever ways you can imagine
and her frustrated at the associated
pointless paperwork generated that
left her GIRFECked and thereby

references what would be
in former times his plain designation:
You know, sometimes I think that
we're the stupid ones!

Karma directs my eyes to the clock, 6.15pm.
And the moment *arrives*, epiphany!
The thankless hours, the cowardly cession
to abject nonsense on daily basis

and a whole evening's work ahead.
My colleague's assertion answered in
deafening trumpet blasting revelation
and for me the distinction achieved;

The stupidest boy in school.

...FASTER, FASTER, MUST GET FASTER!....

Slow down, you move too fast...
You've got to make the morning last
Switch off the router, go net free
Put on the kettle and make some tea
Nana Na Nananana...feeling grooveeey!

Hello, blackboard, what'cha knowin'?
I've come to watch your white lines flowin'
Wipe it clean, it's so easy
Get a kid to do it for free
Nana na nananana...feeling grooveee!

I got no downloads to do
No junk icons to keep
No passwords or spyware that cause me to weep
Put off the projector, the sunshine's for me
And now I love you,...all is grooveee!

Nothing slows your life down

Like super-fast broadband!*

---

* With a hat tip to Simon and Garfunkel.

1. WHAT FRESH HELL IS THIS?

Log into the ORB and report your own faults.

Recent high profile data breaches…
We are experiencing a problem with internet connectivity.
Use multiple passwords as unscrupulous hackers, could potentially
gain access to your PC and sensitive Council information.
As you are aware, the Council's ICT service has been
disrupted for the last two days.

Misconfiguration and was unable to complete your request.

The Council was the victims of a sustained
cyber attack on the SWAN network.
…fault with the desktops last night as
all desktops seem to have the Bit Locker error showing.
All network access that uses an internet-based
connection is currently not accessible.

Denied website error code 1143.

Open wifi access at L&T teaching sites is disabled
while the IT suppliers investigate the problem.
Avoid scams including those purporting to be
from Microsoft technical support.
Note: Start Windows normally and follow
error shutdown recovery prompts

Update your iPads outwith school hours.

DO NOT use the ICT suite until fault is repaired.
Someone deliberately flipping keyboard keys.
…in the meantime watch our short animation
to find out cool future digital plans.
…avoid force quitting and confirm download
security code with ICT support.

Report any suspicious activity to the CGI helpdesk.

...adjust settings that will leave your computer
vulnerable to hacker gangs.
...avoid too complicated alpha numerical codes.
The problem is that when someone uses
the wrong password 3 times on ANY computer
the whole account is then locked down..

...to do a risk assessment type form for every website we use!

There is currently a network issue...
There can often be bugs and incompatibility issues.
Updates often use a lot of bandwidth, meaning
that it may be difficult to perform updates...
...do a test by updating one device first to see what is involved.
...list of problem apps encountered when upgrading...

This is a temporary measure, until we upgrade.

Your connection to the version that is compatible
with your suite of new programmes is outmoded.
Find out at this link:
tOtLLiZzz@nutzformonkies
how ICT is improving learning and teaching
and combatting Trojans in the system.

Council will not be liable for any losses incurred by the recipient reading this.

2. WHAT FRESH HELL IS THIS?

An idea straight out of the 8th Circle*
at GTCS head-quarters;
Teachers to keep a 'weekly
online journal of reflection'[9]

in those spare hours
we teachers have too much of,
Friday evening, for example.
Reflect on the weekly successes

and failures, especially failures!
Consider, ponder, then catalogue
better approaches and
commit to the same, record;

Every. Single. Week .
Asking, *How can I improve?*
Every single week
commit to this flagellation

every single week
this new age Kalifornia style
solipsism masquerading as
Professional Self Improvement.

Think ye of the impact
on your time and sanity
of this degree of introspection
and induced duplicity

as you know your manager
will eventually access the same
and should you be less than
economical with the truth

---

* reserved for fraudsters of various sorts. See Dante's *Divine Comedy.*

your resignation document
written in advance, preparing
(As we say in Scotland),
your own jotters, literally!

Across a career all these words
of reflection like an evil therapy
or a Stalinist era confession
which causes the descent into madness,

the title of your journal
whose degree of introspection
really puts the anal in analysis
retentive to the extent of your

proctologist advising immediate surgery.

3. WHAT FRESH HELL IS THIS?

While some become expert, most teachers become fairly competent in their job after a suitable length of time. When this happens, automaticity takes over and brainpower is freed for performance and creativity up to the level of ability and interest. By not worrying about how to do the job, lightness surrounds the lessons, a force that tends to be catching. In addition to more effective learning, it just feels nice to be taught by someone who knows what they are doing. And if such a teacher is an expert and the pupil a child, often they don't even know they are being taught, so gentle is the guiding hand. Experts naturally become mentors and templates for others. And often they are loved and fondly remembered in time.

Perhaps being an expert is too related to intelligence and temperament to be something that can be reliably expected, but competence can be developed by recognising the essential features of that development. These features are not mysteries and any rational system would ensure that they are locked into the training. But gently, as the gentlest gamer is the soonest winner.

Let's find the right advice. And here it is, in slight paraphrase from the famous Swedish warrior-king Gustavus Adolphus. He's talking about his army officers, but the principle holds for teachers, even Scottish ones;

Let your captains build up their knowledge and skills in incorporation with their own style in a stable environment.

Don't keep changing things, don't keep sending fresh instructions, edit for them the superfluity in their life, it's the colonel's job to protect them from those who would destroy them by overburdening their minds. You gave them the job, let them do it.

Praise strongly, criticise as light advice.

Show them loyalty, expect it back. Let them internalise the drill protocols, victualling requirements, quartermaster administration, the manual of arms, understanding scoundrels, judicious use of the lash, the language and manner of leadership.

There, you see, nearly a 1:1 match with teaching!

And so, the same translated into teacher-talk

Much encouragement, a friendly word of advice.
Don't keep giving them new things to do.
Don't micromanage.
Let them build up their skill sets their own way.
Protect them from nonsense and nonsense traders.
Show them loyalty.
Give them gifts which reflect their professionalism (a nice wheel-lock pistol, an estate in Skåne, 4x cans Superbrew, £5 M&S voucher, etc).
Don't keep giving them new things to do and
Don't keep giving them new things to do and
Don't keep giving them new things to do.

But supposing

you fail to see a pattern in education in the last 50 years,
or are otherwise incapable of learning the lessons you apparently identify,
or are (honestly) indifferent to the fate of schools (your kid goes private),
or actually (honestly)you don't want them to flourish because of some secret female resentment,
then what you would do is follow the opposite advice of old King Gustav Adolf because after all he was trying to be successful,
and so.

We have the current situation:

State of the art lying and self-deception coming from our millennialist masters, their sock puppet managers and embedded parasites within the tinpot Stasi all with a view to stealing your sanity and owning your soul, which task they attack with the zeal of self-deceivers.

Training courses, updates, downloads, warnings, records, responsibilities, boxes to be ticked, the schizophrenic media's reporting, the endless procession of new ideas that aren't really new to be considered and incorporated or rejected and marginalised, the curriculum and school life bent to accommodate the narrative of excellence we all must worship. The eyeballs on the walls, always watching, the atmosphere of disapproval, of disappointment, of skin of the teeth completion, of immanent failure, of failure itself. The dream of escape.

Every. Single. Day.

Your Pain is Their Pay!

Unsurprisingly, the result of this confusion and straight out assault is to undermine confidence in self. The true voice of intuition and accumulated wisdom is silenced by our indoctrinated deference to the marauders who claim to be our experts and advisors. No one defends us teachers and, ashamed of our incompetence, bit by bit we backward scale ersatz Dr Carol Dweck's *Steps to Growth* ladder.*

> I failed
> I can't do it.
> I know I won't be able
> What's the point in trying
> I don't want to know how.
> I don't want to do it anyway
> I don't understand any of this
> I'm not clever enough
> *Ah waant ma mammy, noo!*

---

* One of education's top charlatans. She took a simple well-established banality (teacher attitude impacts on the pupil; *who'd have thunk it!*) and by means of smoke and mirrors tricked the visitors to her tribal tent that she was selling an educational elixir of such potency that after one session children are improved. The Growth Mindset is properly named, check her bank account.

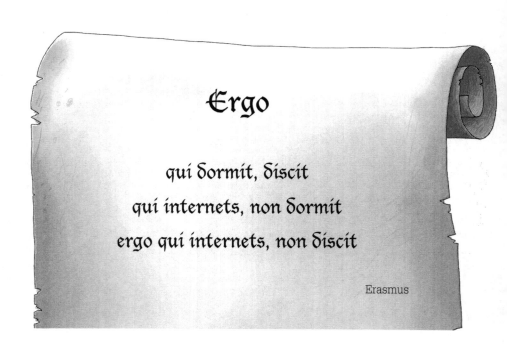

Ergo

qui ðormit, ðiscit

qui internets, non ðormit

ergo qui internets, non ðiscit

Erasmus

IT has been shown to disrupt sleep patterns, especially amongst children. Erasmus was onto it years ago!

For those of ye with yet imperfect Latin: Sleep consolidates memory, technology disrupts sleep, therefore technology disrupts learning.

SHIRLEY CLARKE: SPECIALIST IN FAILURE

also specialising in bad haircuts this
multi-millionaire purveyor of misery through
educational trickery passed off as excellence
and sold to the most gullible, our HTs
and Directors of Education.

Familiar to our monkey ancestors
a simple idea of assessing your pupils
and here fashioned into a club which
with simian enthusiasm she
and her troop batters us

into submission again and again
and…again; books, videos,
training programmes and lecture tours
all nicely costed to ensure
her stash targets are met

without doubt proven excellence
in cashing in.

It's cleverly done, the careful editing
in good old Church of England schools
the willing stooges parroting their faith
to get on the curve and in Shirley's good
books,.. and payroll.

Her story; starts off as a good idea
but then seeing the coin to be made
selling universal elixir and fake treasure maps
to simpleton councils and HTs
she quickly morphed,

as they all do, into a 100%
fake reformer, naturally on joining
that gang of freebooting captains
she became a government adviser;
no more proof needed then!

Granted, she knows her snake oil
from her hair dye bottle
but this knowledge alone does not explain
the success of her travelling fair
depending, as it does, on everyone else's failure.

For this confidence trick to work
years of training are required in
undermining teachers' confidence
in their own skills and judgement.
Reduced to tears

and maxxed out working memory
piling insecurities atop each other
provides the guarantee that no-one
will have the bottle to call time
on this smirking pied piper

unless and until, as you will be,
finally cornered by the snapping hounds
of endless assessment and ever improving
attainment, and unable to multi-task
yourself out of the coming

mental shredding
you lash out in desperation:
Shirley, you've done your job on me.
I don't know whether I'm coming or going
and accept I'm rubbish at teaching.

Now, get the f...out of my classroom!

FOLIOS OF LEARNING

another form of

When I looked in the evidence folder I couldn't believe how great my wee yin was at everything. Gold standard work everywhere. And to think the school had the cheek to complain about him not doing his homework, being disruptive and needing support. Anyway, I think the teacher will be getting a box of Quality Street instead of their face kicked in!

Playground banned parent (appeal pending), Sandwood Primary, Glasgow.

EVIDENCE OF LEARNING QUIZ:

What's the difference between Folios of Learning[10] and just looking at jotters for evidence of work?

Is it:

a.   10 hours

b.   20 hours

c.   30 hours

Answer at foot of page in Swedish.[*]

---

* Svaret är ja, det är a, b och c kombinerat; sextio timmar.

52

GTCS ENHANCING PROFESSIONALISM

Precisely how?

By...

Creating online 'resources'

Whose take-up rate is never revealed

For obvious reasons

And whose net effect

Is to create jobs for themselves

Which generates the sort of evidence they need

To attract more funding for themselves

While making more bureaucracy

For us

And further digitalising our lives

The better to monitor our inefficiency

And waste our time

Crushing our spirits

Making us less efficient

Which leads us back to the top of the list

Don't bother asking how this improves children's learning

As the answer is clear;

Now you're professionalised.

WHEN DOES EXCELLENCE GO TO SLEEP?

Excellence never sleeps and neither will you

if you bed her.

(This will not be the delightful threat

you may think it is.)

PS. Don't worry, no-one else loses any sleep over this.
Or money or promotions.

PERFORMING SEALS

Those with a passion for curriculum change
noticed that excellence was not being best served
in the maths classes of our primary schools;
they found the same old numbers
as were reached by our cave man ancestors
counting magic stones.

After years of so-called progress
one and one was still two
and doubling just gave you four!
The problem was obvious, teachers were
failing to add value, elevate attainment and
bring sums into the 21st century.

And thus a suitable subject for un-inventing.
At best price!
So call in the top dollar experts
using the usual snake oil salesman tricks;
give it a sticking name, like SEAL.*
Then Bamboozle with silly science,

and the fungible concepts of;
emergent, perceptive, figurative, facile.
(Don't worry, no-one knows what they mean).
Present made up statistics for evidence
and let dupes do the same to other gullibles.
Now, let's start this programme with dots;

---

* SEAL = Stages of Early Arithmetic Learning. A counting scheme purporting to help maths
strugglers. Much use of dots and the ever popular little plastic monkeys. Basically, someone
modified well-established teaching strategies after repeatedly mistaking budget vodka for
lemonade, which caused them to see coloured monkeys dancing around their head and moving
spots in front of their eyes. The accompanying manual, apparently similarly inspired, establishes
new rules of grammar and comprehension. This scam comes very well recommended by
its inventors.

lots of them, so you really are seeing spots.
And then, overlapping definitions to ensure
that although you can never be sure wtf
you're doing, there are plenty of boxes for ticking.
Finally, work stations galore (productivity
enhanced, *Ha Ha!*) which we'll call

a 'maths carousel', because the teacher
really will be spinning like a plate on a stick
as they rush between the different groups.
Thus feeling inadequate to the task,
which they are, and so not in a fit position
to call it true until gravity does its job

on the plates. And on you!
And if you ever think of asking
how any of this is better than before,
or how intelligent people could buy into
this micro-timed, micro-managed nonsense,
then don't.

The great and powerful Oz has spoken. Do not arouse his wrath!

Oh,…pay no attention to that man behind the curtain.

RE-INVENTING MATHS

Ladies, I have found a way to solve the staffroom biscuit fund problem. As arithmetic is a subject whose essential principles of learning are unchanged since pharaoh counted his pyramids, I believe that it is ripe for re-invention. I would like a volunteer to give up their playtime tea break to take on this task. Any profits accrued from successful sales of this new scam, sorry scheme, can go to the staff biscuit fund. As a reward, on successful completion of the project, the volunteer will enjoy a full set of classroom colouring pencils, or four cans of superlager, if identifying as a man.

Anonymous HT of anonymous primary school, Drumchapel, Glasgow*

---

* NOTE: The author is currently working on a scheme to double the efficiency of teaching SEAL maths by doubling the number of pupil groups (from, say, 4 to 8), halving the time spent at each work station (from 12 to 6 minutes) and tripling the number of learning outcomes per child per session. Target acquisition and boxes ticked will be increased by an order of magnitude. Indeed, a whole term's learning outcomes can be achieved in a single lesson. And it comes with the added bonus of increasing fitness and encouraging weight loss by the teacher achieved by the necessary rapid transition between the different groups. Courses cost £480 + VAT per session and can be booked at: NExtSCAM @iConnedUwthMaths.com

THIS WEEK'S BUCKET OF GUILT

Pick any three:
Starving children (Africa)
Rainforest tribe's plight (Brazil)
Shoebox Santa: In the Christmas spirit (Africa)
Global warming (whole world)
Poaching rhinos, elephants, gorillas (Africa x 3)
No shoes; Buy one pair, send another to Africa (Africa)
Amoebic Blindness (Africa)
No Fresh water (Africa, Asia)
Goat sponsorship (Africa)
Support ruined schools (Africa)
Flooding (Bangladesh)
IT initiative (Africa)
Fairtrade rice (Asia)
Poverty awareness (Scotland)*
Tigers disappearing (India)
Getting eaten by tigers (India)
No pencils, paper or schoolbooks (Africa)
Leprosy (Asia, South America, Africa)
Polar bears, corncrake, panda, manatee (not Africa)
Africa, Africa, Africa (three times your fault)
Drowning Women (Madagascar)
Everything bad that's left (rest of world)

---

* Special toxic pity workshops have been run for pupils to create posters raising awareness of Scottish poverty. These have then been displayed throughout city schools to reinforce to screaming level the joint message of shame and guilt. There was much celebration among professional guilt-mongers and their embedded cysts at HQ at this evidence of Scotland nudging its way up the victim's list.

GIRFEC GIRFECKED

All the words are just words
by which they transfer guilt
to us in a game of
pass the parcel full of shit.

Guess who holds it when the music stops?

What strange power prevents
the true source of these failed children
being identified?
What special covenant is broken

by saying out loud,
Do these children not have parents?
Look ye to them with your judgements.
And policies.

Why are we teachers never defended
against biology and lifestyle choice?
Where is our champion to step
in front of the hostile mob and say,

Those who are without accountability,
cast ye the first stone.

A SIMPLE GIRFECK UP

Part 1

So, he doesn't do his homework,
ever.
Throws it in the bin
in front of me
spoils every class,
always
I regroup each day, knowing
that I'm having a proxy
conversation with his 'parent'
through him.
Not his fault, perhaps?
He's just a kid and I try to be
an adult
and reach out discretely
his response shows ingrate power
at atomic level
reveals me to be out of my depth
to help him.
As Dirty Harry says,
A man's got to know his limitations.

Part 2

And so,
I help myself by imagining my visit
to the HT's office as
Achilles' tent before Troy
and hear Ulysses calm that mighty Greek's
wounded mind;

Time hath, my lord, a wallet at his back,
Wherein he puts alms for oblivion,
A great-sized monster of ingratitudes:
Those scraps are good deeds past; which are devour'd
As fast as they are made, forgot as soon
As done: perseverance, dear my lord,
*Keeps honour bright.**

Perseverance keeps honour bright.

---

* With a thank you to Ulysses via Shakespeare.

RESERVED IN YOUR NAME WHEN YOU ENTER THE PROFESSION

Death of a 1,000 tiny cuts

Aka

The killing power of accumulated trivial slights

Do not under-estimate how those little insults add up. One day you're coping, the next you're going to work in your pyjamas, tie-dying your hair and talking pish like me.

Jonny Depp, rebel globalist perfume and luxury watch advert-whore and ersatz assassin.

THE TEACHER'S TALE

Leonardo told me that there was a time after he was teaching for about 10 years, this being the mid 90s, that he felt pretty good about the job; he knew the kids, the curriculum, the resources required, had slicked up his lessons, internalised the admin. He had loosened up and was considered a popular and witty teacher. But then his journey to experten status took a U turn. The internet arrives and teaching turns upside-down. A new curriculum, new methodologies, focus on core values, focus on evidence, focus on accountability, focus on the journey to outstanding, focus on reporting, focus on poverty, democracy, anti-racism (in a maths class!) and in all these new foci, the focus on teaching maths was lost. Along with the joy.

Although still good at teaching maths, every year he became less and less competent at everything else. And all these everything elses increasingly became more important than teaching. Eventually he passed on his way down, the fiery comet of excellence on its way up. Poor Leonardo, him backward scaling the ladder to excellence. His outstanding avatar occasionally, fitfully, visiting him in dreams.

At first, with all the talk of journey to outstanding, Leonardo's thinking; where will they get all these fantastic teachers? The 10,000 all singing and all dancing entertainers who incorporate excellence and core values, formidable admin skills and who are driven to sacrifice their lives for their profession? He whimsically concluded that they must be recruiting them further North, or the Orient, or even the nether regions! Perhaps, coming through the system is a new super breed of future teacher, digitally-enhanced DNA replacing the ancient human incompetents.

But seriously, he knows the answer; there are none.

Where then, does all the talk of excellence and outstanding leave the ordinary teacher? Isn't it enough to be simply good at your job; it seems not! But perhaps, when he hits rock bottom and his world flips again, he will see excellence for what it is. The scintillating show was really just flashing electric lights, the presentation the lesson equivalent of a newsreader, 100% haircut, 0% content.

It is a tale told by an idiot
Full of sound and fury
Signifying nothing.

The real survival skill for teachers

is the ability

to live within an irrational and hostile environment; idiot parents, empty management, double agent colleagues, failed leadership, traitor curriculum, crushing bureaucracy, enemy media.

In short, to accept

zersetzung

as your final fate.

In a similar context, as globalist parrot and former shadow FM Kazia Dugdoo noted:

I must say, accepting the inevitability of my ruin was slightly less terrible than I had expected. Indeed, the committee officers themselves noted with approval my calm demeanour as they served my terminate and evict order. To be honest, it was never truly possible to be successful with so many shape-shifting enemies dead set against me. I'm optimistic that broken and cast out will not be as bad as it sounds.

CHILD FRIENDLY ZERSETZUNG

in the event that your children are not over-burdened, stressed and confused please ensure that;

- their individual learning intentions and success criteria for each lesson refer to their personal targets and that they review this upon completion of the lesson by recording it in their target jotters.

- the plenary should be used to share future learning goals.

- they may also record successes or failures in their e learning journal.

- they watch *BBC Newsround* every day to top up on their cortisol levels, inure them to globalist propaganda and addict them to popworld trash.

DAYS OF BROKEN ARROWS

Toy guns, swordfights with sticks, chasing girls
are of the past.
Get over it!

Climbing walls, swinging on branches, throwing stones
all risky undertakings.
For safety's sake, don't!

Movies, legislation, news, 'educated' gynocracy
feed his destroyers and crush his spirit.
Enough, toxic masculinity!

Gender choice, *My trans son wears make-up*, endocrine warfare
You thought you were a boy.
You were wrong!

Depression, lack of focus, withdrawal, delusion, the life online
the planned and fated boys' future,
Sterile, your kind gone. And good riddance!

Fist fights, militant enthusiasms, competitive, impulsive, testosterone
You thought you were a boy, you are.
I'm your Witness!

SLUGS AND SNAILS AND PUPPY DOG TAILS.

It has been claimed that females in general lack the abstraction necessary to understand or sympathise with a male viewpoint. And in particular a little boys need for competition and hierarchy, and that the said female teachers are otherwise hostile (in a usually small h way) to the various ways this manifests itself in interests and social interactions: *I'm drawing my favourite killer robot.*

The solipsism that comes naturally to the female is quite alien to a boy. His thinking is existential in form and function. He lives in a more concrete world of things and movement and risk and doing. He doesn't want to think it through and talk about his feelings. He's not holding back or denying emotion and empathy, he's just not especially equipped for this. This is a feature, not a deficiency. He just wants to know the rules and the parameters. He's a boy, this is how he works. Generally, problem solved, he's forgotten about it already, as he's other boy stuff to do.

Sometimes with the best of intentions, the feminised teacher's response to boys and boys' issues is the exact opposite of what it should be. Failing as it does and should, the feminised environment tends to then **view boys as basically badly socialised girls in need of correction; pink them up.**

Possibly most young, and yet childless, female teachers tacitly hold this view, and how could it be otherwise given the current nature of our society and the cliché loaded unthinking feminist framing that comprises much of the ~~propaganda factory~~ college training that produces teachers. The costs of this ignorance and bigotry are disproportionally and unwittingly borne by our sons in the short term. In the long term, of course, we all lose equally. **Feminist achievement unlocked!**

Obviously to express such views and think you could rationally debate them in a female work environment like a primary school would prove you an idiot with a suicidal bent. If not worse! Luckily, **I'm writing this for a friend who is not me.**[*]

Signed,

Not Me

(author)

* See *The War Against Boys: How Misguided Feminism Is Harming Our Young Men* (Christina Hoff Sommers)

EXCELLENCE HAS A DAY OFF

It starts with the register,
children's names being substituted
for picnic items, fizzy drinks,
sandwich fillings and continental cheeses.
They are not fazed by the switch.

One maths lesson taught with
no reference to targets
children apparently fail to notice
its absence, perhaps they don't care?
Those who finish early are tricked by,

not extra work, but extra free choice!
Playtime extended by ten minutes.
Milk and story time doubled.
Language lesson, no trick this time,
just a promise; finish early, then play.

Lunch over we go a walk in the woods
build a hut, then race back, Last's a…
Next, Shakespeare verses parsed
from say, Romeo and Juliet,
Act out the same, for a laugh.

Project proceeds without children
debating their own protocols, nor
stating QI outcomes, they know already!
Teacher just teaches, flying the lesson
on experience. Somehow it lands okay.

The day passes with no reference
to the conveyer belt of pedagogic
balderdash that clichés our lessons.
No fires, no police, no children lost,
Excellence ends the day with a Beaujolais.

*You know what, Boys and Girls, let's do it again. But don't tell
the head-teacher.*

Chapter 4

Seeing a Pattern

SEEING A PATTERN

Premise: A steady effect argues a steady cause

More digitalisation, interface problems, time wasted; **TEACHING LESS EFFECTIVE**

Productivity initiatives, less productivity, more stress; **TEACHING LESS EFFECTIVE**

Enhanced curriculum content, ineffective introduction, still incorporating previous enhancement; **TEACHING LESS EFFECTIVE**

Pedagogic innovations, not needed, pretend compliance (ignored)); **TEACHING LESS EFFECTIVE**

Visits from improvement officers, confusion implanted, things get worse; **TEACHING LESS EFFECTIVE**

Head-teachers become policy implementers, no school leadership, staff not protected from nonsense; **TEACHING LESS EFFECTIVE**

Commitment to reduce bureaucracy, bureaucracy increased, time stolen from sanity; **TEACHING LESS EFFECTIVE**

New smartboard introduced, unreliable, money and time wasted; **TEACHING LESS EFFECTIVE**

Constant content updates, cannot keep up, don't bother trying; **TEACHING LESS EFFECTIVE**

Complaints about less effective teaching from all and sundry, teachers more stressed, off ill; **TEACHING LESS EFFECTIVE**

Talk about giving professional respect, no professional respect given, the circle squared; **TEACHING LESS EFFECTIVE**

Endless talk of progress and excellence, no-one knows what it means, teachers fail to deliver whatever it is anyway; **TEACHING LESS EFFECTIVE**

Profession nearly exclusively female, feminine and feminist viewpoints dominate, lack of balance: **TEACHING LESS EFFECTIVE.***

Dear reader, if you can see the pattern you are smarter than those who have a professional interest in improving education. Although, perhaps, an 'apparent professional interest' would be the more accurate phrasing. As, honestly, the dysfunction serves the interests of web wizards, academic researchers, professors of learning, ghetto politicos, equality activists, social workers, media managers, NGOs, public purse plunderers, grievance mongers, hysterics, and the flotsam and jetsam of our society's discontents. Some teachers have even had the gall to wonder if all those interested in improving things and delivering services dedicated to the same, might not actually be making the problem worse, or even creating it.

---

* This point was included at the request of a friend.

WHENCE COMES THIS RELENTLESS FLOW OF NONSENSE INTO THE TEACHER'S LIFE?

Let's follow the trail backwards down lines leading from **the very best of intentions** to curriculum innovation, new technologies, pedagogic practice, policy goals, management trends, bureaucratic obligations, media mischief and the societal forces that have brought about general unhappiness now scaled up to discord to find the wicked seeds of our predicament.

Irony abounds at the source in most human enterprises and one would expect a wise man to be aware of this truth and to see the wasteful and disappointing eventual outcome lying entreasured in these weak beginnings, and counsel accordingly. Alas, it is hardly a surprise that the *weltanschauung* of our political masters, social visionaries and bureaucrats contains no such person, and that no-one with any influence was able to see these trends and policies for the future threat they really were and stop to them before they developed momentum.

The weak beginnings found in those lines of ancestry were not necessarily, by and of themselves, idiotic or wicked; however, in their journey to the here and now they have picked up the jaundiced zeitgeist of our age to arrive full of fever, absurdity and hubris. And teacher crushing power.

And so now, too late, we are locked in a Celtic knotwork of trends within trends, lines of causality going off in all directions except straight; but all eventually leading to the serpent's jaws.

And then, the great levelling which will bring the truth again.

HOW TO BAKE A NUTTY TEACHING PROFESSION

Take:

Lots of Women; so that staff will all publically agree and privately plot
State supported dysfunctional 'families' looking for scapegoats
A 'passion' for education among politicians (or some such worded pish)*
Experts experting at public cost

Mix in:

Narrow world of pedagogic reference to ensure that 'new' ideas actually seem like new ideas
A 60 hour + week
Funding without limits sloshing around the heels of freebooters
Chocolate buttons for wages

Next:

An historical trend in which the media has become increasingly sensationalist and contradictory in its ~~reportage~~ straight-forward lies
School mission enhanced with justice
Never make any reference to real world truths about intelligence or race
Replace leaders with policy facilitators (aka Party kommissars)

Then:

Widespread ignorance of the historical European liberal education
The digitalisation of school, private and children's lives
Value, accountability, records, evidence, evidence, evidence
Unsocialised children and parents

---

* see former PM joke duo Tony and Gordon for the highest expression of this sentiment.

Add topping:

Threats from parents
No one sleeping right
Pointless CPD
Private life overwhelmed

Instruction:

Place in classroom and leave for a few years or until nutty crust is apparent. Perhaps some sprinkling of tweets might complete the process
If you want it well done then wait until the realisation that prime (or all) fertility has been wasted chasing a 'career'
Your primary teacher is now complete
Cats may be added at a later date

Serve with wine.

WHERE DID IT ALL GO WRONG?

Historically, the educational template for our modern primary schools was a creation of the deeply learned, but practical, Victorian bureaucrat. Our school buildings, class arrangements, timetabling, curriculum content, funding, professionalised staff, educational intent and ethos represent their concentrated genius. They also accepted as self-evident truths a certain view of children which found expression in a simple curriculum founded on literacy and numeracy, with teaching based on fact and repetition in a disciplined setting. The tacit worldview was traditional and masculine. Schools also strongly represented (organically) the moral and behavioural codes of their day, but did not teach it as a topic. All the add-on content of our modern curriculum was then considered a responsibility of the family or the various church and other institutions and clubs. There were many men in teaching, although women increasingly made up the numbers.

Time passes, things change, the institution relaxes a little, becomes increasingly staffed by women, but maintains its essentially patriarchal outlook. And its curriculum still founded on the three Rs, the Bible and the firmly imposed discipline; all well remembered by the author.

And then, for various reasons not within our current purview, institutional change accelerated into the modern age leading us to the here and now where this original educational style and content came to be seen by progressives as crude, harsh and lacking relevance for moderns. Swiftly, its timeless knowledge store and pedagogy based on fact and repetition was replaced with processes, choice, computerised resources and the assumed relevance of global issues and societal causes.

This replacement, however, this has not been an entirely happy event. And a ghostly presence of pedagogy past haunts us, not just with what was, but what still should be; a simple curriculum and school environment shorn of bureaucratic excess and faddish nonsense. Despite all the efforts to deny it, awake parents and teachers still recognise the disciplined old style as what education should be and that the progressive attack on old school was never honestly based on its supposed lack of relevance or utility, but inspired by other motivations.

Seriously, secretly, no one intelligent believes in the faddish content and child-centric ideology currently dominant in primary schools, and thinking teachers despair how this could have come to be. They know that cause and consequence are hopelessly entwined, but still see the connection between what was lost in the rush to embrace new practices and the decline in teaching standards.

Naturally, as our educational system has spun deeper into cascades of nonsense, complaints abound about the low quality content and output. Thus devaluing the role and status of the primary teacher, from educator, patron and mentor to state functionary in bureaucratic day-care camps.

Teachers become stressed over not being able to deliver what they cannot deliver. And live, although they may not actively consider it so, within an existential crisis. The system tries to address the issue of quality and relevance by further embracing the very forces that have caused the effect; IT, global visions, grandstanding social concerns, psychobabble as pedagogy, feminist framing and bringing in ever more women.

And now, here we are with a golem; bloated, stupid, obsessed with social mission and inflated with hubris. Thoroughly feminine and feminised in its structure, habits, interests and instincts. Its own enemy.

And then, the force multiplier

The digitalisation of school life has brought additional wheech to the vortex of madness which swirls around the teacher. As with all of our other bureaucracies, the arrival of IT has increased the admin by an order of magnitude; nearly all of it as actually real-life useless, as it is apparently vital. All these reports, records, evidences which will only fulfil their proper purpose when they are burned. Of course, as the digital world expanded this nonsense, it increasingly robbed schools of real life lesson resources. You know, things you could access by picking them up and share by handing them over.

The digitalisation of private life has enabled the culture of complaint, surveillance, pointless comment; the creation of a never-resting ether hinterland of malcontents. And happy to spread their unhappiness around the world at the touch of a button.

The digitalisation of children is robbing them of innocence, outdoor activity and silence. Proper sleep patterns, normal brain circuitry and metabolism, age correct references, appropriate socialisation are all scrambled. Alas, ironically and tragically, all the features that are mentioned as the benefits of the digital world to our children's life, are actually the mortal enemy.

And no point here in mentioning anything connected with the long term impact on children's health of microwave radiation swirling around classrooms and contained within the ipads we so vigorously promote!

The government joins the bandwagon

Then the government's emphasis on value, accountability and 'openness' obliged even more record keeping which fed back as reinforcement to the previous trends. This, in turn, empowered and legitimised the culture of criticism and complaint, and the demand for improvement. And this became, what was hoped to be, a vote winning cry because of 'passion' for learning.

Then, in a hubris which challenges the gods, in a curriculum which promises excellence, we find new ambition which further reaches beyond this stellar goal to incorporate a vision of ending world poverty, hunger, injustice, war and transgender prejudice, all by P7. Thus, the world fixed, does Scottish education threaten our progeny with redundancy!

Not a mention, far less an honest policy, regarding intelligence or race or culture or bad parents, or the impact of ignoring this on school life.

The trolls join the posse

Then the rise of the Social Justice Warrior meeting revisionist history, societal amnesia and post-colonial guilt finds its Petri dish in schools. And, willing dupes amongst the teaching staff happy to apply emotional pressure to bend their charges' minds with guilt masquerading as, variously; engaging with the world, being a global citizen, champion of a fairer future and above all, tolerant.

Their never ending commitment to improvement and world justice (aka women complaining), met its happy partner in the i phone. Having an instant mob, the warriors attacks are pitched at the lowest level. It feels great, having the security of the Borg, while safely transmitting your virtue and bravery to the world from the comfort of your home.

If we could get rid of all the expert input and social justice goals that alone would be a production multiplier and increaser of satisfaction quotas. Margaret Thatcher taught us that.

Pocahontas McCrindle , P3 pupil, John Greig Primary School, Ibrox, Glasgow

A SJW SEES *THE* PATTERN

The socialisation of gender within our schools assures that girls are made aware that they are unequal to boys, this being reinforced by using texts that omit or tokenise the contributions of women, language that obligates girls to adopt a men-centric feminine ideal, denies their victim status, blocks challenges to the patriarchy's ring-fenced careers and forces girls to be little homemakers in class, tidying desks while the boys relax or play.*

The Patriarchy in the Primary Class. Professoress Manless

The professoress describes the top 12 problems...

Problem: not enough girls in STEM

Problem: minority girls underachieving in schools

Problem: girls encounter systematic hostility in gym time

Problem: boys tease girls

Problem: girls feel undervalued

Problem: some girls internalise male prejudice and don't like being girls

Problem: girls are made aware that they are unequal to boys

Problem: teachers trivialise girls' concerns

Problem: texts omit women from culture and history

Problem: everybody loves boys and respect them.

Problem: girls forced to do without victimisation support

Problem: who do these boys think they are?

---

* This head-shaking nonsense is paid for by your taxes; enjoy!

…and helps us identify their origin; **the patriarchy**.

…and completes to the solution; **remodel white boys to be gender neutral**.

Until they stand up to the unfair treatment they are receiving, girls will continue to receive an inequitable education and their gifts lost to society.

Professoress Manless*

This is the anti-male agitprop that too often counts as educational research. It is not just a woman complaining. It is not harmless, for it is lapped up like cream by our political retards, funded and then actioned into our educational system. It is the backdrop to your children's education.

Perhaps you would be inclined to laugh at the pantomime crudity of its presented understanding of how an institution, never mind a society works, but this would be to miss the serious psychological and dyscivic impact on your boy and girl child. But you won't be laughing when they turn into little guilt-bots.

Your boy is to believe that he is enjoying privileges unique to his sex, and that this connects to injustice, even tyranny. And he will grow up to be sex bully member of the patriarchy like his father (or erstwhile father); welcome to the gift of guilt! This war on our sons' masculinity is relentlessly waged every day.

Your girl is to believe that she is subjected to constant misogyny, the patriarchy (that's her dad, uncles, brothers, teachers) limiting her world, marginalising her achievements, a denial so powerful and pervasive that she has (as the fembats claim) even internalised it; welcome to the gift of resentment!

Please note that I partly agree with the professoress's claim that our education system betrays girls, but for completely different reasons; their true gifts lost to society, and to themselves, are their most fertile

---

* It's a real quote, I just changed the idiot's name.

years. Too often, what should be the crowning glory of a girl's life is irreplaceably sacrificed in smashing imaginary glass ceilings and chasing other assorted feminist chimeras that are first presented as ideal or even necessary female goals by our primary schools. Check *Cosmo* and *Elle* for examples of lost and complaining, *if I could turn back time* cougar CEOs and various Go-girl champions.

The purveyors of these wicked falsehoods will sacrifice your children to valorise their beliefs. They legitimise the repressed misery of their choice to eschew children and family by sharing their hurt with everyone else.

Their choice at your cost.

Thusly, does the repressed soul seek its own apt metaphor.

PLEASE ENJOY YOUR VICTIMHOOD CAREFULLY

... and make good our campaign promise on improving justice and inclusion outcomes in education by using income saved from teacher salaries and de ring-fenced pensions to fund a policeperson and lawyer in every school.

Scottish Government Justice in Schools Conference, Larkhall Ladies Cocktail Club, 2017 (enhancement @inclusionFU2)

IMPROPER USE WILL ENDANGER YOUR SOCIETY

A CONSULTANT SEES *THE* PATTERN

The apparent problem:

A gender-biased hidden curriculum and
subtle gender inequities in teaching materials
cause uneven distribution of teacher time,
lead to an inequitable education with
boys getting the lion's share, it
takes its toll on girls who (as we know)

are trained by schooling to be silent and passive!

The *only* solution:

So what changes can be made to create
a more equitable learning environment
to give our young women a chance?
Teachers need to be made aware
of their gender-biased tendencies.
and the hidden sexist curriculum.

And the need to confront the patriarchy.

The money shot:

*Education departments should be providing
mandatory gender-equity resource modules*
to in-service teachers, and gender bias needs
to be addressed with all pre-service teachers.
*Educators should be exposed to
properly designed CPD to ensure*

compliance with correct standards.

The real potential:

no scientific proposition need be formulated,
nor evidence presented in advancing this
nonsense with a view to robbing
the public purse, just play on the emotions
and emphasise the buzzwords; *male bias,*
denied our voices, empowering the victims,

that women love to hear!

A POLITICIAN SEES THE PATTERN OF FAILURE...AND IS

Learning Lessons, Applying Solutions

Failing system, stressed staff
scourged daily in media and daily discourse
after listening and learning lessons
politician promises to fix the problems caused

by the previous incumbent.
Experts consulted at public purse
initiatives forced through at public purse
extra courses, admin, accountability

solutions mediated
by the very bureaucracies and agents
that have caused them
which surprise surprise reinforces

the original problem and
causes new ones. Staff still
overwhelmed with initiatives
and regulation and workshops.

More fairness makes (as it always does)
things less fair. More clarity results
in obfuscation, more inclusion gives irony,
hypocrisy and eventually denial.

Teachers scourged again
in media and daily discourse
children's future failed again shock!!!
New politician promises to fix things

caused by previous incumbent
starts by listening and learning lessons
experts consulted at public purse
Initiatives forced through…

…and repeats at public expense. Ad infinitum.

THE ROAD TO HELL

Paved with good intentions but

the law of unintended consequences strikes and

effort seems to go awry.

We see the same pattern every time

our educational system tackles a problem

the eventual effect is the opposite

and this is not a bug, but the essential nature

revealed.*

The simplest way to explain the behavior of any bureaucratic organisation is to assume that it is controlled by a cabal of its enemies.

Conquest's Third Law of Politics

---

* And sometimes it really is controlled by its enemies. ☺

A LITTLE HISTORY

All bureaucracies have a history which follow the same pattern; its invented to address an issue, initially invested with energy and quality staff, becomes powerful and efficient, grows beyond its mission and its ability to effectively manage itself, becomes a plaything for other interests, often outwith the original mission, and even its scope of action.

These other interests add self-interest and security of employment to their mission, resulting in inefficient practices. Morale and output falls. Eventually this is recognised and the scalpel is taken, but to all the wrong people, as the organisation now only exists to serve the embedded interests. And when these finally become full parasites, the bureaucracy becomes a blight on its original mission. But alas, now established for reproduction and self-protection, it cannot be reformed or even shut down.

Like broken Rome in the 5th century, all it can do is wait for an Attila to burn it down and put it out of its misery.

This is how it always is. Entropy applies to institutions and their bureaucracies, as it does to the universe. Things fall apart, the centre cannot hold, mere anarchy is loosed upon the world.[*]

And this is where we are.

The fix then? There is no fix, just get out of the building while you can.

Make your own alternative. It's going to get worse, before it doesn't get better!

---

[*] admitted, the phrase is stolen

EVERY LITTLE THING

Spoiled by the design
Madness of progress
Evidence, reflection,
feedback targets, records.

Even infants are infected
with the contagion
that ruins the lovely event
lost in the moment's rapture

of being personally read to
by the big boys and girls
of the upper school.
The best of ideas

that needs no addition
to complete the perfection
of learning and socialisation
between these two;

loving and loved, wee and big
much better than buddies
in that moment and,
by the necessary form of this,

the heavy hand of idiot pedagogy
powered by loveless jealousy,
whose origin is apparent to those
who can see such,

comes down to ruin the ending:
one group to show evidence
of 'good listening'
at 5 years old FFS, the other

group noting evidence of the same
and so made a spy by default;
our class gestapo preparing
for all our future

by design.

SOME LOVELY GIRLS

O, my crying heart

Call them any name you like
their names are legion
in this woman's world
of existential danger.

These innocent virgins,
whether yea or nay,
reared up for the sacrifice
at the alter of progress.

Naïve as kittens put
in the drowning sack
for, as they think, play
at being grown up.

To be robbed of their beauty
and womanhood, their life's
glory and purpose sidelined
during their most fertile years.

By the poor life choice
of a career encompassing
the personally disastrous falsehood
of achieving equality.

That proves a point
for someone else's ambition
warped by hatred, apparently
against the fictional patriarchy.

But actually against their own
whom they secretly hate
for representing the potential
that negates their childless choice.

And so, they use you to validate
their miserable mistake
by selling you an ideology that
is a time bomb to your future.

And turn you unwittingly
against your own in turn
as you take on the kapo's role
for shame.

Awake, you lovely girls!
Use your female instinct
to sense the deceiver
who snakes among you

disguised as you own.
And see the pattern repeated
in every school across the land.
The choices are clear when

the eyes are open;
a diorama with cats and wine
your fated career planned
or your own beautiful children.

Ave Mater Dei

THE RESCUE ROBOT

Too many magisters have been brainwashed by technology and know of no other system of teaching other than that offered by this force which slaves them and their charges. O, and Carthago delenda est.

Cato in a speech to Caledonian Senators urging the compulsory memorising of epic poems in primary schools.

It always comes to your aid,
when IT problems beckon,
with the promise of a fix.

As claimed by the service provider.

Its presence protects constantly,
a digital Gigantor in miniature,
flying the ether for you.

Against the bad guys and poor connectivity.

You can ascribe it a gender,
name it and pick an avatar for it,
like a six year old would.

Hey, how cool is that?

This personalisation feature
is actually the start and end
of its genuine functionality.

Yet, even as users see it not working

again and again, they curiously
appear not to notice
this failing, such is the strength

of their belief in technology.

A fitting religion for our age
which snares their minds with
infantile baubles

the better to lead them down

the path to the matrix where
the rescue robot appears again
but this time, not to rescue.

And this time, with full functionality.

AND SO IT GOES

We need more experts

We need more programmes

We need more CPD*

We need more digitalisation of school life

We need more wisdom from our political class.

We need more rules and regulations

We need more UN vision

We need more wards of state in school

We need more children who don't speak English

We need more children from hostile alien nations

We need more

And then it was gone.

---

* Continuous Professional Development; a near useless conversion of public money and teacher time to low grade re-education. However, such uselessness is only confined to the practical sphere for their contribution to the framing of the teacher's worldview, self-view, competence and confidence is very great indeed. From the viewpoint of an evil and deceiving masterplan they are a very successful strategy.

For your job's sake, you must publically record them as 'Very useful', 'Interesting' and 'Can't wait to try it out in class.'

CPD is the means whereby our enemy's propaganda department wages a relentless war against teachers.

WELL, WHY NOT BRING BACK THE PAST?

If you can invent a time machine, that might do the trick.

The past is a different country and

all the attitudes, skills, knowledge and mission which informed and motivated our olden days educational system from the professor to the first day P1 are gone and

in the modern world of education, intuition and common sense, plain speaking and honesty are officially out of fashion and so

teachers have few allies in the fight against curricular dysfunction, indeed,

many teachers themselves have became the stormtroopers of chaos as they have unwittingly embraced the statist, globalist, feminist and relativist viewpoint

relentlessly streamed from TV and Twitter feed their whole lives along with the sexualised and anti-civilisational effluvia that organically accompanies it, and so,

having no other world of reference (or interest,..*excuse me while I answer this X Factor tweet*,....they lack the knowledge and habits of thought to resist this nonsense,

far less deliver alternatives because

the past is a different country.

Chapter 5

Fixing the World

FROM WHAT WELL OF GOODNESS SPRINGS THIS DESIRE TO FIX THE WORLD?

What would they have you think, these advocates for justice and 'equity'; that they have a special insight into the world's injustices, one apparently denied to you? And that they have beautiful souls? It must be so, you should conclude, for them to be so moved by the plight of children elsewhere. This is your take-away; bagged up respect, admiration even, at their intellectual depth and moral bravery.

Such goodness naturally turns to action; and thus they are prepared to spend as much of your money as it takes (surely, you would not grudge this) to constantly remind your children of their (especially white) privilege.

They have to do this to your children because they have no children of their own. And they have no children of their own for good reason. Although, even to identify this reason counts as wrongthink in this sensitive and caring age.

Good adults, see the truth behind this faux concern. Consider the mind's construction behind the virtuous face. It is not love, nor Christian piety, that animates these outcast warriors, but jealousy and hatred of your children. Your family. Our society. In their delusional attempt to fix themselves and silence their howling minds, they try to equalise the rest of the world and bring it to their own confused and lonely level. Starting at the source of their own disquiet, the family, they naturally begin their therapy with yours. And especially your children.[11]

The inclusion, the empathy, the tolerance stated and signalled is in fact its opposite. They will steal your child's life. And transfer to them the ironies and hypocrisies that populate their own world of the overthought, overwrought mind. Assemblies, special focus weeks, partnerships, sponsorships, poster propaganda, no opportunity is missed to remind our children of the misfortune of the anonymous others. And our complicit role as parents.

This lesson in guilt will pay back its dividend, as we will presently see.

Children, you have done no wrong. Ignore adults when they talk of the unfortunate life of others.

Parents, doff this constant spiritual and mental abuse of your children, and for that guilt that is no part of them, love your own all the more.

Excepting our saints, the urge to save humanity is too often a false front for the desire to rule.

SWEET DREAMS ARE MADE OF THIS*

And who am I to disagree
with a diva who's travelled
the world and the seven seas,
and found the answer

to the problem with our education.

A lack of diversity, an unfair world
deficient in African studies and
equality workshops, a current fashion
among our SJ millionairetrixes.

An insufficiency of guilt transferred

to our infants which done via
FGM, HIV, and water injustice,
Scotland's excess a cruel taunt
to less happier (and wetter) lands.

We find the blame accepted

satisfies (albeit temporarily) the vaulting
world ambitions of entertainment savants.
Their psychic guilt assuaged
by being paid in kind by our children.

Who am I to disagree?

---

* With no apologies to the Diva. Tbf, excellent song.

UNICEF DAY OF CHANGE

No it's not!

It's just another day

of

guilt.

And oxygen for those.

And income for such as those.

THE GREEN BANNER OF EARTHLY GOODTHINK

Seen by the dawn's early light
occasioned by my early arrival
our flag flying proudly,
they would have you believe,
although ragged, filthy and torn

but not by shot or shell
nor anything more heroic
than simple neglect, which reveals,
as it always does, the truth:
No-one gives a SH…(choose your
disposable waste item)…IT.

Not even the Eco Committee
who fought the good fight
to achieve the Bronze Level flag,
currently coloured like a shoe rag,
which proclaimed the schools'

concern for the Earth, via recycling.
But that was two years ago;
the boxes have been ticked, the
photos taken, the tweets twitted.
The small concern gets smaller

to become finally, like all our
school initiatives, a hypocrisy and
waste of time for all concerned.
This fact revealed by observation
of the general waste skip adjacent

to our flagpole to find it full
of the all recyclable paper
destined not to be!
Our pupil eco committee
meet later today to discuss

a poster design competition
to encourage reducing waste
as ironies jostle for first position.
Luckily, they have no idea of
the power arrayed against them.

Truly, we adults sully them to forgive ourselves our acedia.

DELIVERING EQUITY

If you thought delivering excellence was hard enough?

Turning their faces against God's ordinance
the nameless priests of our religion
of education add a new mantra
to the catechism of excellence

in a decree coming from that
unseen unknowable nether world
wherein they dwell at public purse
we now add delivery of equity

to our daily prayers for inclusion,
diversity, tolerance, rights-respecting,
fairness and global awareness
which by themselves were not,

apparently, sufficiently millennial.
Ignoring the blessing of the moment
these alms thieves yearn for their
fantasy future of global social justice

in which they, by virtue of preaching
a never-ending list of
overleaping demands,
imagine grace shining on them

and by bending an unwilling
congregation of teachers and pupils
to their just will they see a
a grateful future applauding them

to their eternal heroic reward
for their prescience.
Indeed, their future was assured
when *they* reached for the sublime

but forced us to grab the ridiculous
and worship without discussion
or demur at their alter of false hope
they revealed their true face

as self-deluders and aggrandisers,
conduits for *them* who would
destroy our children and so
well deserving of their just reward

but in the Eighth Circle
with the simonists, flatterers
and bearers of false witness,
where the unvarnished truth

is at last admitted on the
point of a prodding pitchfork;
all people are equal
and then they are born.

When you demand utopia

you are served apocalypse.

There is no equity, it cannot be delivered, except as chaos. Oh, s***, the mike's still on…!

...infamous autocue error by John Swindler, Govt education minister

---

* 'There is a Happy Land' speech given to 'Education for Non-male Justice' activists at The Ned's Rest bar, Ferguslie Park, Paisley, 2017

EUROPEAN GENIUS

Recognising immediately the pedigree
of the unauthorised modification
I asked who did it
to be met with silence. Someone thought

they were getting into trouble
for unwittingly demonstrating
the little origin that brought us
on a 50,000 year journey

successfully to the here and now;
the intellectual acorn from which
spread the mighty oak of our
ancestors' achievements

from Solutrean point to i pad: European genius.

K strategy defined by a string and pencil
at 7 years old
usefully (and thoughtfully) added for all users
to log their rewards on the chart.

Am I getting into trouble?, she asked,
still bemused by my adult face.
No, it's my privilege to give you this message:
You are your own reward!

HERE WE GO AGAIN

The Scottish Parliament's education and skills committee has hit out at the poor-quality of education for children. Councils across Scotland are failing to meet targets of inclusion and attainment for a quarter of school pupils, a group of MSPs has said.

(Edited to save you the bother of ever reading suchlike garbage again.)

It said the policy of inclusive *blah blah blah*
OMG is often not functioning properly.
Blah blah represents a 44% increase ☺
of harrowing first hand experiences!!!

Whatever from areas of deprivation who have lower chances
And *blah blah* not get the support they need. ☠
And LOL feel more excluded in a mainstream setting
cultural barriers in some council areas to the policy of inclusion. ✓✓✓

"a lost generation of vulnerable children ."®
blah blah undermining the success of this policy.
FFS with an impact on areas of deprivation,
blah blah blah Government's desire to close ☹

the educational attainment gap. ✓
The MSPs concluded *blah blah blah*
effective inclusion integral to the success *blah*
blah Getting it Right for Every Child policy. ✌

Blah blah disappointing results ☹
education system is simply failing *OMG* ☠
without the knowledge they need *blah blah*
and kids mental health targets missed too!

Amid the revelation this week of declining standards of literacy and numeracy amongst Scottish children and young people, John Swinney, cabinet secretary for education, told parliament that the "statistics need to improve".

Just the statistics!

My advice would be to just falsify the results: Following the well-established pattern and the advice of realist colleagues, this strategy worked for a certain foreign teacher in Sweden.

And this is all you need to know about Scottish Education until the apocalypto!

O, and here's the mandatory cliché, as evidence of whatever which must be introduced into any statement by a government official:

'Education provision needs to fit the child, not the other way around.'
(You may rearrange these words in whatever way pleases you)

IN A NUTSHELL

Fighting for a better world. Part 1:

consider ways that you can promote tolerance

and exclude tolerance to those who oppose tolerance

except those who oppose tolerance to those who oppose it.

Obviously!

Okay, got it.

HOW TO PROMOTE EMPATHY AND CREATE A JUST WORLD[12]

It's easy (if you try...)

1. Take a child whose moral sense is still developing.

2. Show them images of unfortunate others (especially same age kids for self-identification).

3. Remind them that it is their duty to fix this and not the parents, family, nation or government of those children.

4. Ensure that there is no context to any of this.

5. Employ automatons ignorant of 4 as goodthink educators.

6. Repeat message every year in projects, assemblies, action weeks, whole school approaches and Newsround, especially Newsround.

7. Get Madonna, not the holy one, but the idiot exhibitionist, to purchase Africans.

8. Employ juvenile airheads (e.g., half-nude twit, Emma Watson) or seasoned idiot-liars (e.g., wooden-headed, shelf-soiled stick insect, Angelina Jolie) as UN ambassadors for white guilt.

9. Employ local versions of the same. (e.g., blow-up mynah bird, Ginger Spice)

10. Your child is now empathetic and can promote tolerance and create a just world for all citizens (and not just Africans).

Self love, my liege, is not so great a sin as self-neglect.
The Daufin to his father, the King of France in Shakespeare's *Henry V*

SAVING THE RAINFOREST AGAIN

And again and again

aside from some beads
and feathers he is naked
to the eyes which are
as brown and deep
as a mazama.

He is not pretty, but,
note the distinction, beautiful
in a strange way for a child
like a fierce little animal
pugnacious, independent

fitting attributes for his life
in the jungle and
especially his fated future
as his world is swept
into history's bin

to emerge as a colouring book
and a location for a trip
into guilt for our children.
A curious converging of
utterly disparate worlds

their actual and our concrete
jungle yields the same plea
as the magazine cover from
all those years ago: *This child
might live happily ever after –*

if 'civilisation' would just keep away.*

---

* Referencing a *Sunday Observer* magazine cover from 23 Jan, 1981 titled 'This child might
live happily ever after if "civilisation" would just keep away' (see The tribe that won't surrender,
p.30).

SCOTTISH EDUCATION CONUNDRUM

'Helping learners build a fairer more equal world.'

'You shall not bear false witness.'

How do you reconcile the first statement with the second?

Send your answers to:

Big Ride. At least he'll read them.

ASSEMBLY IDEA: LET'S HAMMER SCOTTISH CHILDREN WITH AMERICAN RACE GUILT

A day trip to Montgomery

Out of the past black faces appear
For humiliation or punishment
Revolver hipped white cops
Playing the bongos with
Nightsticks on afro skulls.

In front of our white faces
Theirs panicked, or tear gassed
Ape-shit juju meets triple K for
A buckshot reality check
Clash of cultures, Jim Crow style.

Our representative *little white girl*
And little black boy sit together
In the assembly hall to watch
Flames and sirens, snarling Alsatians
And popping tear gas, sharing (at last)

Bemusement and no context
They know what they are seeing
But they don't understand it
The point utterly lost to them
But the images vivid, and forcefully

Handed down from the screen the
Guilty seed entreasured waiting
In each little white breast
On the brood of time which
I could have told them would not

Find a ground to root upon
Except on you!¹³

THE MOST OBNOXIOUS EMOTION THERE IS:

DISINGENUOUS CONCERN

and now,…

☺ via our UNESCO overlords ☺

(and to great public acclaim!!!)

organically connected to the new idea.

PRIMARY EDUCATION

as a time for radicalisation!

OUR EDUCATIONAL SEERS, AT LAST,
RECOGNISING CHILDHOOD AS HOLDING
BACK ATTAINMENT LEVELS IN RACIAL GUILT,
GENDER EQUALITY, SLAVERY TOLERANCE AND
WORLDWIDE JUSTICE.

THE BIG IDEA

I've heard of hubris, but I don't know what it means.

Anonymous (att. to the head-teacher, Bonaly)

Bonaly One World Week[14]
A whole school policy for tackling injustice

There's nothing like starting with a realistic ambition
of 'working together to build a just, peaceful and sustainable world.'
It's true that even God has struggled with this, but then again God
didn't have
the senior management team of Bonaly to help, or the favourable
pupil demographics that enables the children to
'take action to increase equality, justice and sustainability, locally and
globally.'

Locally and globally;
from Equatorial New Guinea to the bus stop outside Saddiq's General
Store,
is nowhere safe from our infant justice warriors?
Seems not! Anyway, if God can do it all in a week
so can Bonaly, under their dynamic leadership, put to bed;
justice, human rights and poverty,
environment and climate change
and faith and community. Within which topic they can also consider;
'racism/bullying/prejudices and its impact'
Except, of course, to themselves as too white (of whatever hue) and
thus
deserving of spiritual abuse.

And finally we have the Whole School Task©
whose theme this year is Hope in Action
Here the virtue signalling and guilty can and make a Pledge of Hope
which we can use to 'encourage people
(and not just children!) to think about their learning,

'what inspires them and how we can build
a one world culture by challenging injustice
to build a fairer more peaceful world,
fit for our children to live in. '

Yes, think about it!
Done yet?

Think about how these deceiving sincere pledges
of hope cultivate a bed of empathy and insight

from which will flower goodwill to all mankind.

Can you imagine an adult writing this nonsense?

Consider which is more scary to your child's future,
the self-delusion or the hypocrisy behind
the false face of the author (of whatever sex).

And know that this passes for management in our end of days.

Ask about the big idea at Bonaly.

*Ye false prophets, say out loud the real big idea. Reveal the force
behind your need to turn our children to hypocrites before our
eyes. Your real master would be proud!*

A short play entitled:

THE ICE BUCKET CHALLENGE

School playground: Group of pupils witnessing teachers courageously demonstrating how we fix the world in the age of iphones and selfies.

Teacher 1; inspired, principled, compassionate, screwing down her courage to face the lifetime shock of 5L of cold water.
Teacher 2; not an idiot.

Are you sure that you want to do this?
Yes, I know it'll be cold!

No, that's not what I meant.
Well, Obama did it!

Yes, that's what I mean; you and Obama, sharing compassion.
What do you mean?

Nothing, I've got your towel. It'll be over in a second, literally!

WORLD PEACE DAY

We were invited at assembly to think of what we could do for World Peace Day@tm

The children were obliged to come up with the usual parroted guff which we hypocrite adults are equally obliged to approve of.

Here's my contribution:

World Piece Day[15]

I start with two thick slices
of virtue signalling brown bread
spread thick with French butter
thus proving I'm no euro bigot
and then don't add bacon
so as not to cause offence
and perhaps a bombing for diversity.
Then, some 3rd World friendly
certified virtuous tofu spread.
Next, add some moral grandstanding
with organic tomatoes and ethnically
inspired racial sauces to help us all get along.
Imagine this, it's easy if you try,
on a plate with Freetrade free range
gherkins raised without cruelty
that much mocked pickled vegetable
finally finding tolerance and acceptance
in this company, a symbol of our commitment
to a piece you could believe in.
Obviously, it is not my intent to cause offence.

Society's childless outcasts
lead

the charge to..................

TOLERANCE
and
FAIRNESS

(and no free speech to Nazis)*

on   the   broken   back
of your

own children's

EDUCATION
and
WELFARE

---
* that's you, reader!

Getting our priorities right in Scottish education

Edinburgh City Council promoting tolerance and a violence free workplace at school. ✓

EIS fighting racism in education. ✓

GTCS promoting equality and tolerance in all its activities regardless of sex, age, gender identification, ethnicity, BMI, sexual preferences, colour, height, race identification, deformity, sexual orientation, disability, IQ, dietary preferences, body art, mental illness. ✓

SED preventing extremism, developing understanding in all our pupils regardless of culture, religion, ethnicity, bomb risk and FGM home preferences. ✓

HM Inspectors of Schools enhancing inclusion with each visit. ✓

A teaching dinosaur remembers the Old Days

The traditional focus on literacy and numeracy was ruining the necessary development of race and cultural guilt. I remember how bad it used to be before our champion institutions converged on the real problem, lack of tolerance and equity. I remember the gangs of fascist teachers roving around the schools preaching inequality in class and assembly, kicking the sh⑧ out of forward thinking pro alt gender staff. I remember the little Hitlers and embyo wife beaters already well versed in intolerance by P1. And the gender Nazi nursey staff forcing girls to play shops and boys with trucks. I can scarcely bear to think of how deficient our education was in the things that really matter. Kids were leaving schools equipped to enter the workforce or join further education without the slightest pang of remorse or shame regarding race or sex. It was terrible. Thank goodness for the GTCS, EIS, SED, City Council and our united political parties for bringing all this to a halt with lashings of tolerance and empathy and no free speech (or employment) to Nazis of whatever gender identity or sexual orientation. From then onwards it's all been puppies and rainbows, to be honest, she-he said.

JUSTICE AND RIGHTS...

Ours is an age of nihilism and atomisation and faux concern. We disguise our neuroticism and confusion to ourselves by dressing it up with fantasy future rhetoric and talk of unprecedented connection Lucky for us that we have social media to keep us sane.

Mark Z, CEO Skynet Industries

All these words.
With their message of injustice
and victimhood and guilt.

What happens to us when they fall on our ears without end?

There is something perverse in human nature
whose origin lies in our remote past
as a survival mechanism,

this rejects direct attempts to control

our thoughts and actions by
embracing its opposite.
Often unconsciously.

Thus we meet the paradox of direct action

which encourages its secret opposite
until such times as it can reveal itself
for what it always was, but until then

and by the necessary form of this its

hidden self manifests as guilt
and hysteria
and hypocrisy.

Is there anyone who doubts that

the UN's rights respecting achieves
nothing for children's rights
but

...the lies with which we are held in submission.

Another successful project rolled out

We hope these projects never end, beg teachers to party leaders

Child poverty awareness training is to be rolled out to all schools in Edinburgh following yet another brilliantly successful pilot programme run by city social workers. This welcome news was revealed at the Increasing Childhood Poverty Conference held at the Balerno Daycare and Addiction Rehabilitation Secure Unit, Edinburgh.

Working with the usual Quislings the project raised awareness of the scale, causes and impacts of child poverty, without mentioning stupid and selfish parents, welfare system gamers, parasitical immigrants or the various scamsters chasing public funds for themselves under the guise of public altruism or policy research.

In the past people used to be discrete about their poverty, but now that there is no dignity in making do or even doing without, the report into the pilots makes key recommendations into what practical faux actions could be taken by schools to make school more affordable for families on low incomes, such as providing free TV packages and lager vouchers, or replacing school uniforms with £100 football tops.

There was massive demand by teachers for CPD events to raise awareness and the incorporation of poverty projects into the curriculum. This was felt to be especially necessary because people in Scotland have zero awareness of poverty as our media and politicians never refer to it. And of course raising awareness of things always leads to more empathy which inevitably results in the problem being fixed.

"Juicy Benderton, acting head teacher at Willhood Primary School, said the project had changed the culture of her school with everybody enthusiastically talking about poverty all the time, even the boys who normally just play football and vandalise the toilets:

"The impact of the project has been huge as staff, pupils, parents, carers, foster carers, seconded social workers, residential care staff and attached security personnel, community police officers and even the local neds have changed the way they think about poverty. They now realise that poverty doesn't just affect children in Scotland, it affects pupils in schools throughout Africa too. No one knew this before. Now the whole school is poverty positive. And we have taken our first steps towards eliminating poverty throughout Willhood."

She continued:"We have made lots of changes this year such as providing free Sky boxes, microwave chips and burger meals and Go Fund Me trips to places like McDonalds and KFC. We give toe-rag parents more notice of school trips so they can plan ahead financially by borrowing from local cash flow entrepreneurs. We have encouraged our wealthy families to donate cast off clothes and bin bound PE kits for families who choose to spend their benefits on catalogue bargains or various juices. The posh children love seeing their cast offs worn by their unfortunately parented peers. Idiot parents can also be supplied with completed homework journals to save them the bother of having to read with their kids or otherwise help with homework."

She further claimed, "It's not fair that posh kids get support at home. These posh parents should experience poverty too!" To that end the school has recently introduced a Poverty Day in which parents are encouraged to let their kids sit up all night watching XXX videos and then send them to school dressed like street arabs and without a breakfast. Some parents so embrace the spirit that they turn up late and drunk for their kids. Other schools have looked on enviously at this successful pilot and plans are afoot for a city-wide introduction. This shows the city-wide commitment to tackling poverty and injustice.

We look forward to returning to the school next year to witness the end of poverty in Willhood.

Read more at http://fourthcolumnnews.org.uk/tfn-news/city-schools-to-teach-children-about-poverty-instead-of-maths-and-english

THE WOMAN'S REPORT ON EDUCATION

We are betraying young women:

GTCS spokeswoman at the Drink Your Kegs Off Conference, Club 18-30, Magaloof, 2016

- women are let down
- women are not given a fair chance
- women feel bad about themselves
- women are patronised
- women are marginalised
- women are deliberately excluded
- women are held back by the glass ceiling
- women are objectified
- women are mocked for displaying their sexuality
- women are victims
- women are made fun of
- women don't get a chance to speak
- women are forced to adopt patriarchal feminine ideals
- women are having to justify themselves
- women are not fairly represented in the astronaut, prison population and garbage collection professions
- women are looked at that way
- women are looked at this way
- women are forced to make sandwiches

Who do these men think they are?

We need female strength to challenge the patriarchy and it has to come from the bottom up. What have men or boys ever done for society?

81[*] year old female supremacy advocate, professional narcissist and on stage nudist, Cher.

Where women are concerned, change should come from the bottom.

Sir Mick Jagger

---

[*] Real name Hilda Ogden; for her actual age in dog years multiply by 7.

THE WAY TO DO IT

Whole School Policy

We realised that we were just ticking boxes. But what we needed was a whole school approach to recording evidence.

- Whole school policy √

- Recording evidence √

- Children not just ticking boxes √

- Sorted √

THREE TWEETS, TWO TWITS

Tolerance and Attainment in Action Conference,
Edinburgh City Chambers, 2017

Three tweets received and shared with the conference floor:

No tolerance to the patriarchy and no free speech to white men.

Madonna, not the holy one, the idiot exhibitionist

O baby, o, oo, ooo, let me cum and o baby baby, oo, let's have sum fun.

Miley Cyrus, 16 year old multi-millionairess nude prison-tatted vacuumhead victim of the patri-
archy, aspiring US president and Madonna (not the holy one, the idiot exhibitionist) acolyte

I speak as an empress, autocrat and above all, woman. Do not allow these half shaved female demons any power over you or your children. They will not allow your child to aspire to any virtue which cannot be shared.

Catherine the Great, Empress of Russia

Harry Potter's bird lashes out at primary schools

The madness worsens, she claims

In a volte face as stunning as it is surprising, Potter's crumpet silenced the audience of growlers, fanny men and feminazis when she spoke as a switched-on grown woman rather than juvenile sock puppet.

Primary schools, she claimed, have more women in them than a nunnery after lights out. And worse, the staff are empowered not by love of Christ but a different mania, love of feminism. Grace, wit and charm, femininity's handmaids, are replaced by division and exclusion and revenge masquerading as equity, tolerance and justice. The impact of this unspoken mania on boys is never considered. And the devastating effect of this on little girls is celebrated as a goal; femininity, matrimony, maternity, our women's complimentary role in creating Western Civilisation, are replaced with false equivalences, victimhood, and unnecessary ambitions which in turn encourage physically and mentally ruinous careers when we sacrifice our most fertile and glorious years for the eventual nothing of a career.

The highest and greatest roles of our sex are mocked and marginalised for so-called careers against a fictional glass ceiling. I see the women who have done this to us, and I know their rotten angry hearts.

We turn our girls into silly little parrots like I used to be and our little boys spirits are crushed as oppressors. As a graduate of Hogwarts, I know the black arts when I see them.

For goodness sake, I beg you, she implored, never let children watch Newsround.

Emma Watson, 16 year old former UN Ambassador of Female Equality

RAISING AWARENESS OF CHILD POVERTY

The project demonstrated that by raising awareness of child poverty, which affects over 21%* of young people in the capital, we can all make a real difference when it comes to tackling this issue.

With a higher level of inclusion and more sustainability in the poverty outcomes, which were ring-fenced with a raft of capacities linking to excellence, we have already seen them attaining improvements in delivery of successful citizenships for all our disadvantaged young person of all genders and orientations. This is all the proof we need to move forward with enhanced funding for wokshops. Our partner institutions at the forefront of the fight for justice and equality, the GTCS, EIS, EDC, SED and HM Inspectors are already involved in consultations with expert lawyers at the UN for translating our poverty targets to policy. We can safely say that the raft of school wide policies we have initiated in raising bomb awareness, slavery policies, tolerance, empathy, anti-radicalisation measures and identifying FGM and sexism has led Scotland to boast that our enhancement of delivered inclusion is unparalleled in outcomes for poverty. Our commitment to CPD workshops will ensure that this enhancement can be conformed.

ECC Slavery and Human Trafficking Manager, Larkhall Lager Festival, 2016

---

* Author is currently seeking a more precise % figure.

RIGHTS RESPECTING SCHOOL

It's bad enough having the pope on our case, now it's the...ing UN too.

J. Ratzinger (class teacher) Prince William of Orange Primary, Bellshill, 2016[16]

A proposition: Is there any evidence that having a Rights Respecting School does anything more than zero?

Yes, there is! Here:

Wrongs Respecting School

Following UN directives to protect
not children but their rights
parents not being sufficient anymore
nor teachers able to guarantee
what has been known since
the beginning of time

lawyers kindly wrote in all down
in 54 articles subsequently translated
for natives of every hue and IQ,
hopefully they were paid
for this service to mankind! And yet
still we ask: *In what way*

does saying 'rights respecting'
make any difference to not saying it?
Are our children's rights not our duty?
And as this duty flows from love
its absence reveals 'rights' for
the bingo buzzwords they are.

We ask then, *By what right, do the*
UN Lightbringers usurp this from us
or hand us the obligation
to find they make their own rights[*]
But, as they shall not love our children,
to what end this concern?

What lies beneath the veneer
of wordy philanthropy whose scope
is the whole world and your classroom.
Let's parse this empowerment zone,
such as we are able, and see
what we see.

Granted, we accept in advance
that the face presented to
the world by UN justice drones,
either salaried from bottomless coffers
or cost-free useful idiots, are actuated
by nothing worse than stupidity.

But they are the false shop front
of apparent good intentions by which
the puppetmeisters, hostile to
your native happiness,
disguise their power over you
and your children.

Which, thus taken, empowers and
legitimises still further their mission
of define and control of our lives
eventually to codify for future action
against bad faith actors;
which means, eventually, you!

---

[*] The U.N.'s Universal Declaration of Human Rights states in Article 29, section 3, that: 'These rights and freedoms may in no case be exercised contrary to the purposes and principles of the United Nations.'

But firstly, *Cui bono?*
We follow the shekels to find it
leads back to the nest of the black
gowned crows as it does
every single time.
Still more recursion

unveils the guilt and hubris
and reverse racism that inhabits
this realm of the unseen,
and deeper still the desire to claim
for themselves control of the story
in which you may enjoy some grace

as a victim, but in which you will
eventually be cast as a villain.
And in making normal the culture and
language of the politically correct,
and the striving after justice goals
whose inevitably frustrated outcome

weaponises our children against us,
and their own world, to become
the policemen and lawyers of themselves.
Eventually our rebarbative regression
through the corridors of the mind
(and the UN building aka mission HQ)

leads to the basement where we come
to a counterintuitive discovery this is no
useless waste of our money
and teacher time, but a long game
played to win the minds and souls
(especially, souls) for the new world order.

Thus revealed in this dream
the joker puppetmaster behind this
assault on our rights and wellbeing
steps out to our full view.
He wears a joker mask.
Who are you and what do you want?

He takes off his mask to reveal
…another joker mask.
His answer, *You know who I am.*
You know what I want.
The smile behind the mask is palpable.
He knows he has won.

'And thus I clothe my naked villainy
With odd old ends stol'n out of holy writ,
And seem a saint, when most I play the devil.'

Actually, Joseph XVI's actual quote was: *Non contra*
nos volo papam et unitum nationes contra nos.

THE INEVITABILITY OF GRAVITY

As we climb the ladder of escalating demands of equity and tolerance
We ask, what is the endpoint
And when will it be reached?

To even ask the question is to intuitively know the answer
We realise instantly that the advocates unwittingly stand
in opposition to us and our families.

They are historically ignorant
And future blind
And not self-aware of their role.

Except for the chosen
Their core value is Nihilism
Their aesthetic is destruction.

Which philosophy rounds to chaos
The lies pile ever higher
The truth is gravity.

Accepting this, after the fall you find yourself cleaner by dint of the
cold air's rush.

A POLICEWOMAN (AS SELF-IDENTIFIED) AND LAWYER IN EVERY CLASS

Monday morning, 9am, P4, PM Kazia Dugdale Primary, April 1st, 2030

Good morning, Boys and Girls!
The lawyer steps forward with a document
You are not allowed to say that, it's discriminatory.
She nods to the policeperson

who steps forward with my open cuffs.
**I am placing you under arrest according to various articles
of the UN Code of Children's Rights.**
But…

…and for resisting arrest.
Two SWAT officers come in and I put down my pencil
The children are surprised, but reassured by the officers' firearms.
And their laser indicators, illuminating my various targets.

Your rebel days are over…!

The taser cracks and I fall with a heavy thump.

CLASS WAR

In the end,

The disingenuous concern

The global vision

The hysteria for justice

all the debate peels away to reveal,

our little girls banished from her true self

our sons denied and replaced

common sense, honesty, prudence, analysis abandoned

the war on the family.

EDUCATION FOR PEACE

Setting euro stab records
chibbing our way across acres
of faces, following on from
our famous ancestors' necessary
example of the same

makes us Scots uniquely qualified,
apparently, as peacemakers
so concluded by top dollar
curriculum advisors who pass
the baton smartly to us teachers

to complete this possibly
slightly overvaulting (*D'ye think ?*)
learning outcome, even for
the Curriculum of Excellence,
given that the subjects

of this suite of lessons
was not punching schoolboys
or even claymored rival clans
but the ultimate goal
of our Scottish Chamberlains

PEACE IN OUR TIME

The great eternal clash of cultures
Rome against the barbarians
in all their myriad modern forms
brought to Pax Caledonia:
Right yous two, calm doun!

And laid at the alter of the
Curriculum of Excellence.
Surrendered and redundant
the former violent world's
violent paraphernalia

from suicide vest to AK to
satellite guided missile.
Likewise, the former sounds
of discord replaced with equally
loud hosannas singing the praises

of the visionary virtuous
Curriculum Consultants who
first proposed training our pupils
in imaging world peace
and thus silenced the critics

while proving themselves
worthy of their fees.
And, O, the humanity; for who else
would have thought it, that
the beautiful world we want

for our children could be delivered
by CPD, policy research, expert input?
But then, alas, like at Belshazzar's feast
reality arrives with a bloody injunction
appearing on the wall;

Si vis pacem, para bellum

THE GENDER WARS

Seen on the school menu:

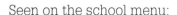

Shepherdess Pie

'Now that's' a pie I'd love to eat', said the bishop to the dinner lady.

'And so you shall, Your Grace', she smiled in response, '*after the children have left.'*

Strike one to the girls. ✓

Chapter 6

Passes for Management

PASSES FOR MANAGEMENT

You need a special type of person to be

in educational management.

You might think that it is about leadership

and wisdom and professional pride

in mission,

but actually...

(HONESTLY), IT'S JUST ABOUT GETTING BY

It's just a day job within a bureaucracy.

With the correct sort of talent, (administrative functionality, departmental savoir faire) one can rise up to one's level of competence, or, if the Peter Principle is accepted, two notches beyond this. It hardly matters, as todays' educational leader, whatever regiment they are in and wherever barracked, are seldom leaders in the commonly accepted sense; of, you know, leading. For example, by example; the first sword in the attack, the first shield in defence!

Now they are conduits for some other colonel further up the food chain. Just pass on the orders, ensure compliance, navigate around complaints, and don't get any big ideas about principles or concern yourself overmuch with the trajectory of our current curriculum or questions regarding the nature of the education you oversee,

...if you want to meet your pension intact!

1. WHAT YOU HAVE TO DO

Is...

have the ability to cope with absurd amounts of administration.

not be too curious, and certainly not challenging, about the utility of new pedagogic or any other new school initiatives. And know not to ask for evidence-ever!

follow orders without question.

keep on the right (that is, left) side of the Twitter and Tweet Gangs.

bend the knee to social justice pieties.

be willing to NOT stand up for your staff, regardless of how stupid the complaint or complainer.

uphold mediocrity and celebrate it as achievement.

regard colleagues as yet unrevealed enemies and discard as required.

never reveal your true face.

never admit you don't know or may even be wrong

be a woman.*

---

* This also applies if you are actually a man (by birth sex).

2. THINGS YOU HAVE TO SAY

Luckily, there are lots of policies coming on rafts, apparently. Just pluck them off as they float by.

Aim for justice (AiJ)
Steps to Growth (StG)
Sustainable future (SF)
Global vison (GV)
skills for tomorrow today (SFTT)
engage staff and stake holders (ESASH)
successful experience of change and improvement (SECI)

vulnerable children protected (VCP)
fit for purpose (FFP)
driving forward standards (DFS)
no child left behind (NCLB)
claiming ownership (CO)
celebrate the world (CTW)
equalities of outcome (EOO)

promote equality and diversity in all its activities (PEDA)
gender sensitive (GENSEN)
empowering females regardless of initial genders (EMPFE)
confront prejudice and stereotypes (CPS)
transgender positive/negative (TRANSPOS/NEG)
commitment to wider achievement (CWA)
improvements in attainment (IMPATT)

positive destinations (POSDEST)
excellence no longer good enough (EXNOGOE)
close the attainment gap (CAG)
Helping learners build a fairer more equal world (HELP)
support Global Citizenship in the classroom (BSHT)
Every Child Succeeds (RBSH)
Fairer outcomes for disadvantaged (FOD)

(These examples, although hopefully exhausting, are not of course intended to be exhaustive.)

Hopefully, such the progress, enrich, develop and enhance (PEDE) mindset will lead to professional values to ensure positive impact. (PVEPI)

Fortunately, all these things you have to say are self-parodying; so there is no need to supply your own.

Although a sardonic smile never gets wasted in this company.

3. DEMONSTRATE STUNNING INSIGHT INTO EDUCATIONAL PROBLEMS

For example:

Children from poorer backgrounds lag behind their more affluent peers.

Professional values ensure positive impact.

Bullying harms the bully as well as the victim.

We need to teach the skills of tomorrow today.

Enhanced diversity improves enrichment.

Inclusion is the key to success.

Children who struggle at school can suffer from low self-esteem.

Please feel some sympathy for the poor arrow of causality; it has no idea which way it is pointing!

4. THIS IS A JOB THAT LENDS ITSELF TO...

- a careerist, or someone otherwise attracted to the power of office (sic) or the genuinely large leap in salary.

- a delusional person with respect to their qualities and abilities.

- a young and naïve and propagandised female who steps on the ladder thinking she is climbing up the way, while proving something positive about women.

- a foxed-out lady who has missed the baby boat and has no other way of justifying herself to herself.

- a dweller in Middle Earth with their antique sense of obligation and mission, possibly even vocation. Such a person would be, broadly speaking, insane. Possibly, they may not exist.

- a ticket-puncher who has a plan to get out (good for you, the sociopath is always the clearest thinker!) when their pension is maxxed with the minimal effort.

Either way, success for the head teacher consists of regarding useless admin, box ticking and following absurd orders not as existential issues, but simply as practical requirements; easier than working and less hassle than caring.

A RECENT JOB ADVERT

Needed: Head-teachers and local government educational officers

- Do you have the ability to follow orders without question.

- Are you the sort of person who is indifferent to the welfare of your staff.

- Are you willing to preside over (figuratively, of course) time wasting courses made by make-jobs at HQ

- Are you not cultured or otherwise indifferent to your native culture.

- Do you have the ability to cope with absurd amount of administration.

- Do you like irony or are, alternatively, insensitive to it.

- Are you passionate about our leftist pieties regarding inclusion, feminism, diversity and multicultural vibrancy.*

- Are you basically indifferent to the impact of policies on children.

- Do you like wine.

Then we want to hear from you

Would suit careerist and/or alcoholic.

Short-term pension boosters, ducker and divers and SJWs are particularly welcome.

A cynical willingness to exploit the rhetoric or complete absence of any consideration as to their actual meaning or final implication is equally suitable

5. WHAT ABOUT THE BROAD GENERAL EDUCATION?

Yeah, what about it?

The BGE was stomping about making a lot of noise recently, but he's been put back in his place and redefined as;

Knowledge about:

- *X factor* contestants

- *Come Dine With Me* contestants

- *Britain's Bake Off* contestants

- *Wife Swap* contestants

- *Love Island* contestants

- *Strictly Come Dancing* contestants

- And ~~the glories of European culture, be they scientific, engineering, arts~~, the Twitter world of assorted celebrity narcissists and airheads

6. AND LIVE IN FEAR OF

Being overwhelmed before you get out.

Afraid of being exposed as an apostate.

Your conscience, which in occasional private moments feels like a judgement on Judas.

Actually being the fraud you strongly suspect you are.

Losing the grace and favour of the parent Twitter gang.

And this above all else to thine own pension be true.

Polonius's advice to his aspiring HT daughter, Ophelia

7. FINAL FATE: BURN OUT

Some just disappear, and are quietly known as 'the disappeared'. A colleague described what happened to one;

It was as if she got a call that her house was on fire or something, she just stood up and suddenly said, 'I have to go now.' And just left the building as she was. This was strange as there was a lashing gale outside. Even stranger, she had nearly completed the school's new gender bullying policy which was left on her desk. She's not been seen or heard of since. Is she ok, do you think? Luckily, the school was sent a supply HT from their Asian multicultural outreach programme. And they are learning English quite well.

And so, even the most constitutionally lazy and resolutely indifferent to the demands and implications of their role are eventually brought to heel (burnt-out, resigned, retired, secondment, medical discharge, undisclosed or just disappearos) by the relentless daily cavalcade of futile correspondence, bureaucratic mismanagement and pedagogic nonsense.

Rumours abound about the disappeared. Some say that they go to some land far to the west. It is claimed that pictures have been seen of them on Instagram, apparently retired in some tropical place, always with a Pina Colada in hand, possibly the same one!

I'm sure exceptions exist. Exceptionally.

CLAIMING OWNERSHIP OF TEACHING

Admittedly he was talking about a spitfire
But the principle holds for anything
After 15 years of flying it he knew
he'd mastered it. Ownership claimed.
Even if the wings fell off, I could still land it.
Exaggerated, but basically true!

Admittedly, he was talking about maths
Said, *After 15 years of teaching,*
there's nothing it can do surprise me.
Systems, plans and resources in my DNA
Pupils encouraged, corralled or excluded
As required, *Each day in class belongs to me!*

And then, the internet, repeat prescription curriculums
Twitterers, fake pedagogy, and school
forgets one mission and gets another
Social justice, equality, inclusion
(In a maths lesson!) the head teacher morphs
From leader colonel to party commissar

The class lesson now in the cockpit
Dials, buttons and levers everywhere
Then the oxygen cuts off at angels 25
Things go fuzzy, can't think straight
Is that the lesson plan or the flight map?
The engine coughs and splutters

And so do the pupils…
Turn and bank indicator canted 45°
Although class floor still seems level
Guns jammed, or is the e-pen not working?
Compass spinning, lesson stalls, wing dips
Then dives for the drink

Loosing ownership

I open the canopy, struggle out trusting to my parachute. Without a doubt,...

Ownership lost.

THE HT LEADERSHIP CHALLENGE

Part 1: Level of ridiculousness vs Salary

What level of ridiculousness in curricular content, pedagogic practice, bureaucratic excess or political interference would lead you to say, 'Enough' and refuse to impose this upon your staff?'

At £60 K plus per annum, none!

Part 2: Models of leadership template vs Just following orders

What template of leadership style and method do you follow? The examples can be current or historic, e.g. Boudicca, Catherine de' Medici, Napoleon, General Model, Teresa May, etc

HQ tell me what to do and I make the staff do it. Anyway, with risk to £60 K plus per annum, none required! Ich folge nur aufträge.

Part 3: Unique ideas for your school vs Standard girly clichés.

Tell us about the special ideas you have for your school?

I want to make it a happy and hard-working team journeying together to improved learning with fun and laughter along the way to justice and equity for all (restrictions apply to certain categories). These are the unique ideas that justify my £60 K plus.

Part 4: Future vision vs Empty pieties endlessly repeated?

Tell us about how your personal learning and reflection has influenced your sense of education's trajectory and destination?

Pupils leave empowered by visions of justice and equipped to enter the big digital multi ethnic café of the future with all the skills of tomorrow today. My personal future vision is £70 K plus per annum.

Part 5: Loyalty to staff vs Pension?

Tell us how you would defend your staff against the various busy-bodies, mischief-mongers, slanderers, Twitter fiends and psychotics amongst the parent community?

The staff don't pay my pension.

HENRY V vs DHT KIRSTIE

Part 1: The Learning Powers of *Henry V**

[*alarums, figures running to and fro, the king as primary school teacher, guards, servants etc*]

Assignment: Underline the king's learning powers.

At playtime nothing so becomes a boy than
running fast and football.
But when the lesson bell rings in your ear
then imitate the action of the scholar.
Summon up the blood and disguise
playtime zeal with hard favoured focus.
Then lend the eye a radiant aspect
let pry through the window of the skull
like a stained glass tracery.
On on, you noblest students!
Dishonour not your mothers.
Now attest that those whom you called fathers
did beget you, be copy now to classmates
of lesser level and show them how to grammar.
And you, good middle cohort
who always try your best
Show us here the mettle
of your pasture, let us swear
that you are worth your completed homework
Which I doubt not, for there are none
of you so lazy that hath not learning zeal
in your eyes.

I see you sit like greyhounds in the slip
Straining upon the start
The games afoot, follow your spirit and upon this nod
Cry 'God for Harry! England and Saint George!'
Then complete your assignment.

---

* With acknowledgement and apologies to the bard.

Part 2: The Learning Powers of DHT Kirstie

[alarums, children running to and fro, HT as the simpleton king, DHT as the king's fool, primary teachers, dyslexics and chained ADHDs with guards, peanut allergy emergency staff, defibrillators, restraint jackets, etc]

At assembly, nothing so improves a child
As Barney, that purple dinosaur of candied
American goodness

Mark this, his words of wisdom
Ye nursery infants to yon outgrown P7s
And too his wagging bum, which adds to
the charming relevance of his message
Of learning powers

Whose exact nature I wont bore you with
by repeating. As I'm sure you were
listening well, as Barney instructs!

This is 21st-century Youtube
Learning culture at its very nadir
Metacognition

In this world turned upside-down

Remember too, his dino friends
Harriet have a go, Tommy never too tired
Queenie never quits, Eric for excellence

Be like them and hold these costumed clowns
Forever In your head, as a constant reminder
To always be better, for there is

No escape from excellence, thus
Be the adult now. You can always be
A child again once you've grown up

I love you.

[as an aside to the audience]

By these hollow cyphers shall I rule them.

Their addled guardians in no wise fit

to oppose my psychobabble.

By such means do I pad my folio

of evidence, whose sheet by nonsense

sheet, paves my path to the highest office.

And theirs to Barney's lair!

THE NONSENSE OF LEARNING POWERS: A TRAGEDY

[Whole school assembly: 23rd April, 2016]

Here's wisdom enough to warrant execration.[17]
On this day, his 400th anniversary, no less!

The teacher's word of encouragement and censure improved with clipart characters which represent, so they are told, 'learning powers.' Like super powers, but better.

And (allegedly) a vital 'metacognitive' quality to which they must subscribe if excellence is to thrive. *Does any girl or boy know what this means? No; well, let Barney the purple dinosaur explain:*

Stunned to stupefied (and I hope, ironic) silence by Barney on this day of Shakespeare, the children watch the giant screen while his (?) powerful presentation and empirical evidences advanced by the effluvium of Youtube seem to do the trick

of replacing the personalised, private word which used to be the subtle heart of good teaching, with more box-ticking, internet sourced, Americanised, weekly-focussed, targeted stock exhortations

by which we transmit to our children the relentless message of ever improving standards and the same management-speak gobbledegook that is ruining us adults

with success measured by virtual approval from internet avatars, all the better to prepare them for their life online.

This monkey level pedagogy of dot connection crudity fails to hear the real message which is instinctively heard by the children all the louder for not being said;

You are not good enough

[then, as he is magic after all, Barney goes off reservation and steps out of the screen and into the hall, 400 children gasp then gawk while he exhorts them with an extempore speech inspired by Shakespeare's day]

But more good children;

Ye know, as we know,

that when you are invited to agree with us adults that you are, by diktat, thusly better engaged and owning of your own lessons,

we adults (for I am really am adult in a suit) are not really asking you, but tacitly telling you to agree

with us that these false flags of truth are clear signals.

You sense, Children, that it is *our* deep need to be seen to be better engaged,

not yours, that powers this nonsense, for why ye cannot yet fathom,

but by matching our dishonesty in asking, with yours in duplicity by agreeing,

we find, alas, the one learning power actually transmitted;

hypocrisy.

CLAIMING OWNERSHIP OF LEARNING

I'm six years old. I like puppies and getting chased. I want to work in a sweetie shop when I'm big.

Claiming ownership
not of a toy car or Loom Band,
which actually can be owned,
but of your own education. *Now,
doesn't that sound good in P2?*

As befits a resident cliché
this 'claiming of ownership'
is not to be achieved through
just good teaching, but
by something much cleverer

that starts life as a simple idea;
'The lesson's purpose should be clear.'
And then force fed steroids
until it becomes a monster with
its own pathology of delusion

and road rage against the gainsayers.
Compliance measured in sleepless nights
even for the useful idiots who
are differentiating 'I Can…' statements
in the wee sma' hours (that's me, btw!).

These self-training monkeys (still me!),
too clever for their own good,
reveal their own insecurities by
prostrating themselves before
the big idea of the moment and,

not having studied humans,
it must seem quite natural
to top and tail every lesson and game
with targets, outcomes and success criteria
revisiting the same during the lesson

to keep children's minds relentlessly focussed
for their self-assessment jotter
and nailing the lie with propaganda
'all children are discussing their work
and how to improve it...' *Ay, right!*

'Even less able children are enthused
by setting their own targets'.
(Apparently). In reality,
the children do their best to ignore
this pedagogy with ADHD,

or brace themselves to their duties,
until limits reached, they face-plant.
In the future, they will come to understand
that their teacher did not hate them
they were just unequal to the system.

As we cascade deeper into
these hybrids of nonsense
we wonder; Is there no champion to rescue us?
Then she steps forward, far the wiser
for being more a human .

I'm six years old, I just want to play.

And, at last, leadership found.

MY LEADER

Understands what she is doing; reads the true meaning, intent, implication and destination of the various practices and agendas that supersede common sense;

or she doesn't know what this means!

Provides wise and spiritual insight;

or cannot!

Is a lightning rod for the staff;

or a conduit for effluence!

Understands that emotional energy sustains morale and regards as vital her role in ensuring that staff do not waste this finite resource overcoming bureaucracy, complying with mandatory nonsense, and other counter-productive pressures;

or has enough on her plate without having to bother about other people's problems!

Understand that many social goals cannot be pursued directly and indeed, by the perversity of human nature, become unachievable when made explicit. Wisdom shows that therapeutic efforts designed to confront prejudice and stereotypes actually end up reinforcing them;

or they think they are challenging stereotypes, leading learners to justice, and bringing us into a brave new world of tolerance and kindness!

Understand the banalty of learning theories dressed up in neuro speak and hold this counter-intuitive, anti-scientific psychobabble at a safe distance to protect vulnerable younger staff from becoming stuffed with this fluff;

or they are unaware of the checks and balances in proper science; the open debate, the peer review and all the other accounting systems which block nonsense from being accepted. They tacitly accept as correct that criticism can exist in only one form; toe the line or blow!

Either they know pap when they see it;

or they actually believe in learning for justice, skills for tomorrow today, reflecting on my targets brain based learning, growth mind-set, etc.

Is aware of the irony of an organisation devoted to raising confidence, positive destinations and celebrating achievement (a happy learner is a successful learner) and yet fails to support its own staff with the same;

or feels that some generic collective word of praise (usually given when someone else is present to better reflect on the supposed gratitude of the leader) is sufficient for the year.

Has integrated mission and loyalty into her selfview;

or, *prima ballerina*, regards her staff as backdrops whose purpose is to ensure she will always look better in comparison. And constantly assesse their utility, and employability, on this basis.

MANAGEMENT LETTER TEMPLATE

I'm sending you this note to say…

- *I was never fond of you and see no reason to change my mind.*

- *I note that there is a train to Glasgow every 20 minutes. Use this voucher, with our compliments, to find yourself on the first available.*

- *You are to be sacked and replaced with a robot, effective on receipt of this.*

- *I don't like your recent haircut, please leave the building until it grows back.*

- *This would perhaps be a good time to consider another career far from teaching. Ulan Bator is nice at this time of year.*

- *Don't hurry back from your mental illness. I'm sure that we'll cope. No, we really will.*

MANAGEMENT FANTASY LETTER TEMPLATE

I'm sending you this note to say...

- *I think you're great because...*

- *Everybody thinks you are a wonderful teacher and so do I.*

- *Please accept this packet of doggestive biscuits as a thank you from the staff.*

- *I know that you've worked like a monster this term: I recognise and salute your achievement.*

- *Thank you for punching that parent.*

- *Your maths class is funnier than a pantomime.*

CAN TOO MANY WOMEN EVER BE A BAD THING?*

The founding vision and habits of our primary schools, while originally male-centric, have so long been feminised that few can recall an alternative. Likewise the staffing, currently at 95% female.

As per the plan for our institutions, women enter and men leave, but things have not got better with this demographic shift.

It could be contended that this lack of institutional yin-yang contributes to the sick body of education, as we see. However, most primary teachers, although if pressed will pay lip service to the 'need' for more men, in actuality don't care and don't fully understand what they are missing by the absence of masculinity; presented, as it is, in our feminised times, as a scourge.

And even fewer would (could?) seriously regard the (their) overwhelming female presence and influence as a major factor in the decline of the profession's status, efficacy and relevance. Such a topic cannot be discussed nowadays, and (btw) good luck with getting funding to study it!

Some teachers are aware that their female natures, interests, social vision and management styles have locked themselves onto a runaway train which can only be stopped by a male engineer. But these sensibly function like a quiet man in school, fearing exclusion from the hive and disapproving tweets should they ever mention this. Probably, it's all too late anyway, male presence or not. Besides, a massively feminised workplace, with a male-hostile hinterland, is not an attractive setting for a normal thinking man.

So fix it yourself, Girls. Superman won't be along soon.

As Nicola said to Kazia and Ruth:[18]
I know we girls have mucked it up, but there's no way we will admit that. Especially to a man!

---
* The title is obviously intended to be rhetoric. And the answer, obviously, no.

Chapter 7

The Nature of the Beast

MISSION STATEMENT

Onwards and Upwards
To the brightest heaven of invention
another set of superlative lessons
brilliantly delivered
to enthralled pupils.

O for a muse of fire
To help plan the next set
to be even better.
Scaling the ladder of excellence
to ever headier heights.

Until gravity lost,
the teacher drifts
into space, and relief
where no-one can see them
face-palm.

THE CLASH OF IDEAS TO EXPLAIN OUR EDUCATIONAL PREDICAMENT

- Institutional stupidity

- Personal incompetence

- Social trends

- Hostile cabal

- Tech addled teachers

- Misdirected funding

- Think tanked to death

- Embedded parasites

- Feminised frame of reference

- En route to Hell in a handbasket (see lesson plan)

Pick any ten from the list.
Rank them in increasing order of importance.

Govt to spend £300 million on educational evil

Fulfilling on their promise to spend more on education, ministers pledged your money to IT system wizards and the various pet projects of tattooed globalist activists.

Ministers denied that this was more of our wealth squandered, claiming that this was the final step that would take us through the gateway to the sunny uplands of justice, tolerance and educational excellence.

Isabella: *Have you ever noticed that the real beneficiaries of all these new initiatives are the ones who propose them. I wonder why that is?*

Katerin: *Yeah,... and for that same money we could probably get a packet of Skittles every Friday for the rest of the year. What a waste!*

[eavesdropped infant playground conversation]

HOPE AND CHANGE YOU CAN BELIEVE IN

Cancel and tear to pieces that great bond which
keeps me pale.

Full to the tits with the toxins
of educational witchcraft
and the sounds of Jack-booted Nazis
stomping around inside our head

we turn to the stated benefits
of our new creed
of multiculturalism and inclusion
to reaffirm our beliefs

in helping learners deliver a fairer
and more tolerant world (And who
would dare disagree with that?)
we find not just female genital

mutilation workshop opportunities
of the merriest kind, but
bomb evacuation procedures,
anti-radicalism training and 24/7 security.[19]

But also, when fairly considered,
our British colour-scape formerly
being too white, the benefits
of red trucked in with diversity

to a road near you to re-appear
as drama on TV news.
Beats talking about the weather
over your ethnically inspired takeaway

And for all this, all you surrender
is some British history and culture junk
thousands of years too old
and an unprotected life

Light thickens and the crow makes wing to the rooky
wood.

AN INSPECTOR CALLS

Prepare your folios, let me my comfort find
Hard word shall fly like dust before the wind
Teachers maun do something for their meat
An so maun inspectors

Cry aa you want, your tears are wine to me
Your *Dinny kens* I hear as music sweet
The judgement already fated, the report
Your punishment, my swinging club

And yet, I deserve your pity
For at that time when all are judged
We wha judge are judgit the harshest
The hypocrite's H branded on the arse.

*They've evolved to be like this. Don't be too hard on them, we're
all parasites on something.*

HM Stationery Office (Inspector of the HM Inspectors of Education)

...and in my dream methinks I saw the world as it should be, as firstly ordained.

HM INSPECTORS OF EDUCATION

Driving up standards by example with every visit

The inspectors lined up before the assembled teaching staff. Their leader, the Kommissar Kapitan of Education, spoke: "*We are going to show you how we've earned our stripes. Me and my officers are going to come into your classes at random and show yous how it's done. People ask us on what authority do we swoop down on you like fiery archangels? Well, you see this,* and he indicated a black cross hanging from a red silk ribbon around his throat, *this tells you that I've earned the right to lead by example and am not afraid of your opinion.*"

He continued, "*We'll deliver to your classes pacey, engaging and light-hearted lessons, properly differentiated and with effective use of technology. You'll see difficult pupils properly managed and led to instruction by subtle psychology. You'll see the pedagogic overload and clichés discarded and replaced with intuition and experience. The rubbish bin will be bursting with the once fashionable nonsense of learning intentions, growth mindset, success criteria, self-assessment, revisiting strategic goals, time to reflect on their target, the chaos of active learning, etcetera, etcetera, blah, blah, blah and blah! The children will start the lesson but lightly burdened, and end it just the same.*"

"*All you need do is watch. Take notes as you wish. Be not afraid of our example, as we in turn are not afraid of your judgement.*"

I me thought; 'Now wouldn't that be something, an inspector that builds rather than destroys, has craft rather than guile, has integrity rather than a checksheet.'

And then a voice said, 'I have sent this phantasie through airy realms to shew ye the nature and scale of your trial in inspection-land. And too, how great shall be thine reward for conquest over this enemy. '

'But now, the dawn beckons, and alas, reality.'

A short play entitled:

THE OPPOSITE OF THE MIDAS TOUCH

HT: Why are you here; we had an inspection only a few years ago?

HM Inspector of Education: Ask not for whom the inspection tolls. It tolls for thee.

HT: Can you not just give me the judgement without having to bother our school with the infection, sorry, inspection, that way you'd still have the fail, but we would miss the stress?

HM Inspector of Education: Ha, ha, you're very witty, I like that in a failed candidate, and I'd love to be able to accommodate your request. But I wouldn't be doing my job if I just failed you without an official visit. You see, it's the official that makes the visit a failure. And it's the visit that makes your failure official.

HT: Do I have any options?

HM Inspector of Education: Of course, there are always options. You can be off ill with stress, you can join the 'disappeared', or you can take the Roman option and use your department issued pistol.

HT: Which one allows me to keep my pension?

HM Inspector of Education: Only the Roman one, sorry.

HT: Ah, weel, everything has to have an ending. And I was never fond of the Curriculum for Excellence anyway. One of us had to go.

HM Inspector of Education: Hey, nice attitude to educational change. I'll put that in the report. And no hard feelings.

HT: None taken, nor intended. Goodbye, cruel world.

[*Exits stage left. A gunshot follows.*]

HM Inspector of Education: God forgive me, but I love this job.

Report Card

HM Stationery Office report on HM School Inspectors

I will return in 6 months to check your continuing excellent progress towards inhumanity and uselessness.

	Primary School Inspector	Grade	HM Stationery Office Comments
1	Cause misery	A+	The mere thought of your visit, even if likely years away, brings long lasting feeling of dread and helplessness.
2	The insolence of office	A	Never having to justify yourself or face consequences for your actions places you in the top tier of contumely.
3	Your recommendations are obvious, ignorant or wasteful	A	Total waste of time and money. Inter department champions.
4	You don't make things better	A	We all know this although we only can say this privately.
5	You are part of the problem	B	See embedded parasite.
6	You know the truth about yourself	A+	You pretend that your recommendations have resulted in improvements and are essential to maintain standards, but privately you realise that you are the very essence of the institutional malaise.
7	The oppressors wrong	B	Very much enjoyed, however, the occasional disingenuous apology downgrades the mark.
8	You are not forgiven	na	At £70 K plus, obviously, YDGAS.

GTCS

A bad case of FFS!

With two feet did it jump aboard the gravy train with its various initiatives to 'maintain standards', 'bring the profession up to date' and 'equip it with the globalist values of tomorrow, today.'

All the fixes are bureaucratic,

all involve themselves as service managers,

all exceed their natural remit,

all operate beyond their native ability,

all further embed the problems,

all will fail as,

all the teachers are not equal to their schemes

and

all the consequences of the repeated failures

will repeatedly fall on the teachers and pupils.

for ever and ever

FFS!

Thank you for visiting us. Please return again soon.

The voice of the educational establishment is not just passively stupid, but poisonously so. Suggest discuss GTCS initiatives in Circle Time.

P5 pupil Harry T, note placed in class worry box

EDUCATION HAS ALWAYS BEEN AN ENGINE

...of and for social change. But the social change was an effect of the acquired knowledge contained within the academic content and then taken out into the world. As such, it was organic and commensurate in size and consequence with the host society.

In our time, much academic content has been replaced with social message. The directness and crudity of this message of course fails in its purported purpose, but it brings down via wasted time, compromised content, redirected energies and the necessity of enstupidation of teaching staff, all other learning with it; as we see daily. Each step in our backward journey from knowledge was predestined when the egalitarian pledge was made.

The fantasy mission now embedded in our curriculum, we await the future vision and social change on which it is predicated. The allotted future will mock our hubris as it curses our stupidity.

The true future will enjoy the smash and crash, it is too stupid to care.

NEWSROUND[20]

How do I hate thee? Let me count the ways.
I hate thee to the depth and breadth and height
My soul can reach;

Teacher dupes building brand loyalty
for TV news with 7 year olds
prepping them for the correct attitudes
of tomorrow today, as defined by the BBC.

Apparently, just what they need nowadays!
More screen time in the toxic digital world
of the adult, honeyed up to sweeten
this bitter pill by child friendly 'fun features'

like the pronouncements of sexed up
teenie UN ambassadors fighting for
women's equality while semi naked
or a cruel puppy trader exposed by

by a brave boy band, thusly
product placement as news features.
Legitimising the lifestyle choices, dress
manner and posturings of celebrity airheads

while embedding deep into
this innocent limbic landscape
the essential features of our Gen Z;
the drug addiction to the screen,

surreal jump cuts, emotions feminised
the validation of the pop world,
the fawning over attention whores,
poptarts showboating compassion

in Versace and 6 inch heels. Easy lies
and socially destructive delusions
presented as truth to gullible young,
Politicians have promised to...

delivered with demonically easy assurance.
The focus on selected nonsense
and ephemera balanced with
the forced filling of defenceless minds

with event and tragedy that reinforces
their narrative of world truths, normalising
the madness of the media with
every episode, encouraging fragility;

Click on the links below if you're upset!

masquerading as concern and support
by making little neurotic dependence bots
(subliminal message-you should be upset!)
out of formerly robust innocents

creating future clients for pharma
but inuring them to their future truth
as TV addled drones by state monopoly,
an implacable enemy in a squeaky voice;

the Newsround newsreader.

...but don't worry, everyone will be looked after!

I hate thee with a hate I seemed to gain
With my newfound saints. I hate thee with the breath,
pain, tears, of all my life; and, if God choose,
I shall but hate thee better after death. *

---

* Thanks (and apologies, if required) to EBB's superlative, How do I love thee? (Sonnet 43)

HANDCART TO HELL TUITION

PREPARING YOUR CHILDREN FOR THEIR FUTURE

As the world of adults tumbles ever into Hell, why not bring the whole family?

Our schools can prepare your children for the adult world with all the features of that world that we love; self and peer assessment, reviews, development conversations, evidence folders, attainment scores, enterprise initiatives, gender sensitivity, skill sets log, race adjustments, setting their own (non-football) goals, reflective journal, endless claims for sympathy for other people's welfare, violence prevention mentors, the digital world, globalised learning packages and, of course, news, news, *Newsround*.

By the time their school education is complete your child will be well equipped with ignorance and guilt enough to lead them to their allotted fate of irrelevant degree, job in a booth, further debt and cultural shame. Perhaps even gender confusion if the education has been especially thorough.

Well done, us!

THE STAKEHOLDERS

It is inevitable that the name
would be an absurd and vacant thing
the pompous jargon employed
by the usual politco suspects
of such obfuscating nonsense.

But really, unknowingly to them,
the idea planted, irony on irony,
by Athena that wise goddess
to mask its true purpose
until the day

when, suitably hammered, into the crypt
comes our educational Van Helsing
to deliver to the living dead thing
that is public education
the final liberating blow

that is a grace to it and a blessing to us.
And find the stakeholders,
at last revealing who they really are,
already waiting in place and holding
the sharpened stick above the black heart.

Ah, Doctor, we've been expecting you!

Notes

1   For example, tolerance or little boys being masculine.
1964: I will not tolerate a child being rude to an adult.
2016: Thomas exhibits an aggressive streak in games. Worryingly, he wants to be a soldier and already shows an unhealthy interest in swords and guns.

2   GIRFEC: Getting it right for every child. The education warrior's version of the Marine Corps mantra of 'No wounded left behind.' Some educational colonels, safely ensconced in a chateau far from the classroom front lines, may imagine their goodthink has delivered success. Others know better that the slogan in reality makes us hypocrites and betrayers, as well as setting up class teachers as the fall guy for the failure.
The Fermat's theorem of educational science; how is 30 minutes a week, GIRFEC?

3   A poorly constructed wall in a modern school in Edinburgh suddenly fell down and tragically killed a child. Many schools similarly constructed had their pupils decanted to other older schools built at a time when they knew how to make walls that stayed upright. The relocation, effective while the problem walls were fixed, was a major undertaking and reflected well on all concerned. Although, the pupils relocated were naturally very disappointed that they didn't just get the time off school.

4   Female Genital Mutilation, Individual Learning Plans,…blah, blah, blah,…
7.65mm Walther auto pistol.

5   GTCS: General Teaching Council for Scotland. Formerly a simple creature, but lately suffering from such an excess of excellence that it has become, through its various self-serving councils to simpleton-government ministers, a blight. A perfect example of mission over-reach!

6   WALT and WILF: 'We are learning to' and' What I'm looking for'; a fad in pedagogy whose exponents believe that learning is almost impossible without these being made explicit again and again,…and again. Naturally, in order to further inure our children to clickbait, these are presented as little cartoon avatars. In real life there are many ways to make an intention explicit. And sometimes, o the apostasy, you don't even need to!

7   Why should boys have got lashed with the benefit of a maxxed out effort, and the girls a little pussy paw token? Boys enjoyed corporal punishment at, minimally, double the rate, and a belt force disparity of at least double too. Equity demands a like for like with school crimes, and so, Professoress Manless is

currently working with the GTCS and the reparations department of 'I've Been Naughty Too', a feminist inspired complaint group who are trying to determine the corporal punishment NOT received by Scottish schoolgirls with a view to demanding the century long shortfall be returned. Girls just want to be properly belted too. Ladies, enjoy your equality.

8   *The Belt Room*: a collection of poems portraying Scottish primary teaching '60s style.

9   I am amazed and know not what to say! This was actually proposed; this is the level of future thinking with which teachers have to contend.

10   Folios of Learning: collected evidence of a child's learning across various topic areas. Brimming with excellence and happy photos they have been claimed by cynics, although not me obviously, to be the educational equivalent of budget holiday brochure. Some have suggested, although not me obviously, that the folios are actually manufactured by a race of elf-like creatures during school holidays or even teacher-slaves moonlighting as pupils. This would suggest, although not by me obviously, that the better the evidence looks, the less evidence it actually is of learning. But who could believe such a thing? Obviously, not me.

11   One could almost be forgiven for thinking that there is a dark undertow to this female concern; Like Goody Putnam who accuses Goody Nurse of witchcraft because her children died of plagues and agues while Goody Nurse's thrived; confusion and anger turn to jealousy which is voided by the accusation. We must be equal in suffering, your child sacrificed for mine or the mine I didn't have while I was breaking the glass ceiling!

12   The crudity of this thinking beggars belief and shows no understanding of real world economics and ethics, or children's emotional development, nor any wisdom regarding unintended consequences. By this thinking, the child is inadvertently considered as a sympathetic adult woman, whose empathy flows from seeing or being told about unfortunate others and which has as a consequence the desire to help said others; or, more properly, to be publically seen to help said others by virtue signalling and shaming realists via tweets and lady street marches. The assumed long term effect of such emotional appeals to the child are enhanced sympathetic development, altruistic behaviours and a love of global justice. The ethical equivalent of joining a three dot picture to make a square.
How a child actually understands and processes this information is not considered, nor that a six year old boy is not an eleven year old girl, and yet both treated as one target in this mental health attack. The adult concern may well be experienced by the child as perplexing and guilt. But you can't just slide guilt onto someone's plate without a context, for then you set up a pathology which

cannot be catharised without the accepting of a guilt for the event you didn't cause. Welcome to the world of the adult social justice warrior!

An unintended outcome of forcing sympathy, naturally never referred to, is the development of contempt; the hard hearted, but realistic, close relative of compassion.

13   See Warwick' speech in Henry IV Part 2: Act 3, Scene 1, for the best expression of this insight.

There is a history in all men's lives
Figuring the nature of the times deceased,
The which observed, a man may prophesy,
With a near aim, of the main chance of things
As yet not come to life, which in their seeds
And weak beginnings lie intreasurèd.
Such things become the hatch and brood of time,
And by the necessary form of this,
King Richard might create a perfect guess
That great Northumberland, then false to him,
Would of that seed grow to a greater falseness,
Which should not find a ground to root upon
Unless on you.

14   This is a real thing. Yet again; I am amazed and know not what to say!

15   For those non-Scotch, or otherwise unfamiliar with the Scots vernacular, a piece is a sliced bread sandwich. Traditionally, it contained just butter and sometimes jam too. Best served flung out of a window to the child recipient in the back court below.

16   Now you know why he left his day job. The former Drittes Reich Flakhelfer (and occasional pope) is genuinely missed. Please come back and banish that smiling anti-Christ; and deliver the admonishment and ban in the church's true tongue. You've got to love a pope that can lay down the bull in Latin!

17   Perhaps this is a typo for execution! Who would've thought that probably the greatest writer ever would disappear down the memory hole on his anniversary to be replaced by Barney? O, the sublime irony; I fancy, in that undiscovered country, Ben Johnson buying him a pint of wine, and the two having a laugh at this.

O, in that assembly, to be vouchsafed a bare bodkin that I may my quietus make!

18   Feminist tragi-comedy grupp who also happen to run the Scottish government with zero intellectual and spiritual leadership. Actually, with zero everything!

19   You couldn't make this up, comedy that writes itself. From the staff advice sheet:

If you see someone suspicious inform your line manager, school security@ or the police. If you suspect a package may be a bomb or similar device DO NOT attempt to investigate or defuse it yourself. Follow step 1.

(In a Scottish primary school, the school security team is either the girls' netball team or the P5 Eco committee.)

20   *NEWSROUND* NEWSFLASH!

We've had lots of tweets from you about how Tommy the Turtle is coping after the sad death of his tank-mate and best pal, Freddy, the fish with a friendly face. Freddy tragically died after accidently confusing plutonium pellets with his playtime snack. Scientists are still trying to work out how to relocate Tommy without upsetting him. They need to do this to help him get over the loss. Although, good news, he is eating again. And we've just heard that Nell the Nile crocodile is looking for a new mate, perhaps this could be Tommy? We'll keep you informed of his progress.

Engineers have developed a new app that helps you do your homework while playing your favourite game. Unlocking achievement levels needs the correct answers to your homework, but don't worry, they have a talking vacuum cleaner bot to help when you get stuck. Now you can really do your homework, tidy your room and have fun at the same time. Takilla Paratha investigates for Newsround.

Scottish school eco committee plans to send used and discarded pencils to Africa have hit a hitch when it was discovered they were being traded for kidnapped baby monkeys. Mizz Sturgeon, the leader of The Scottish Government, and a champion for whole world equality, has promised to become involved and buy back the monkeys with new whisky flavoured pencils. It is hoped to fly them to Edinburgh where they will live in a special monkey refugee camp next to The Scottish Parliament until such time as they get full citizen status. Problem solved thanks to our MPs in Scotland.

ALSO AVAILABLE

WILLIAM WALLACE

Scotland's Patriot

A biography of this crucial figure in Scottish history. By examining the medieval context, illuminating the bloody background of the War of Independence and reflecting on his actions and mind-set, a true portrait of Wallace steps out of the mists of legend.

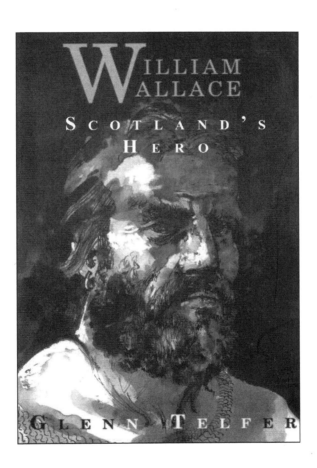

QUEENS OF THE REICH

The 21st century Scottish primary school considered in verse

If you set out with the objective of destroying our education system you could not do a better job than that achieved by its champions and managers. This collection considers the counter-intuitive, anti-human initiatives and other social trends which have undermined primary school education and delivered the exact opposite of its intended goals.

Queens
of the Reich

c F e

THE 21ST CENTURY PRIMARY SCHOOL
CONSIDERED IN VERSE

GLENN TELFER

See other Big Ride titles at www. glenntelfer.me